Orange Grove Goes to War

Orange Grove Goes to War

A Boyhood in 1940s L.A.

Gary A. Glenn

Columbus, Ohio

The views and opinions expressed in this book are solely those of the author and do not necessarily reflect the views or opinions of Gatekeeper Press. Gatekeeper Press is not to be held responsible for and expressly disclaims responsibility of the content herein.

Orange Grove Goes to War: A Boyhood in 1940s L.A.

Published by Gatekeeper Press
2167 Stringtown Rd, Suite 109
Columbus, OH 43123-2989
www.GatekeeperPress.com

Copyright © 2022 by Sara Jotoku
All rights reserved. Neither this book, nor any parts within it may be sold or reproduced in any form or by any electronic or mechanical means, including information storage and retrieval systems, without permission in writing from the author. The only exception is by a reviewer, who may quote short excerpts in a review.

Copyright for image on front cover: iStockphoto.com/archello74 (Gated community houses with palms).

Library of Congress Control Number: 2021941996

ISBN (paperback): 9781662915468
eISBN: 9781662915475

Introduction

As my father approached his mid-seventies, he looked back with renewed interest on his childhood years in Los Angeles. He dug up old photographs, reestablished contact with grammar school friends, clipped articles on the history of his native city, and probed his own memory. An inveterate record keeper, my father carefully filed the results of his research in manila folders, which were soon bulging with interesting facts and stories. It dawned on my father that his findings might be of interest to a wider audience, and he resolved to compile them into a memoir.

The initial motivations for my father's efforts appeared to be a sense of nostalgia and a fond wish to reconnect with old friends. However as long-dormant memories resurfaced, my father became increasingly preoccupied with reconstructing the events from a few key years in his youth. In particular, I sensed a need on my father's part to explore some of the most painful experiences from his childhood. This was rather out of character for my father, who typically maintained a cheerful demeanor and tended to avoid situations involving emotional difficulty. I believe that the process of researching and writing this memoir was cathartic for my father and enabled him to come to terms with events that had been bewildering and traumatic to him as a young child.

The harrowing episodes in my father's memoir are offset by lighter moments of joy, humor, and even suspense. The characters – relatives, neighbors and schoolmates – range from tragicomic to heroic, and include a number of classic Los Angeles archetypes. The book also includes matters of historical interest that are not widely known to the public. The rich variety of experiences and people portrayed in my father's memoir, along with the mixture of personal and factual topics, I think make for a particularly compelling and engaging read.

My father originally envisioned each year of his memoir as a separate book, but for the sake of continuity, I have combined all three years into one book (the last year existing as a fragment). The original prologues and postscript for the first two years have been retained as they provide insight into my father's evolving conception of his memoir. My father continued adding new content to the third year until just a few days before he passed away at the age of 81, dictating words to family members when he could no longer put pen to paper. It was my father's wish that his memoir be published after his death.

One disclaimer: the events depicted in this book took place several generations ago, when sensibilities were different from today's norms. Some viewpoints and terms expressed in the book may strike current readers as dated or even offensive. Some of these outdated views my father disavowed within the memoir, but others he let stand without comment. Since I can no longer consult my father about this content, I have chosen to leave it as he wrote it.

A number of friends and family members took the time to read Gary's draft memoir and provide invaluable feedback, while others offered the emotional and tactical support my father needed to keep writing. To the following people, a heartfelt thank you: Don Glenn, Janis Glenn, Jean Twomey, Dan Ogilvie, Hilary Hays, Astrid Dodds, Bob Oliver, Marlene Oliver, Sonia German, Emiko Katsumoto, Winnie Blatchford, Amy Smith, Gordon Ellis, Jan Olsen, Bill Rutledge, Charlotte Horstein, Scott Horstein, Evelyn Glenn, Antonia Glenn, and Patrick Glenn.

If I have neglected to acknowledge anyone who provided support for the writing of this memoir, my sincere apologies, and know that my father appreciated your contributions.

—Sara Haruye Jotoku

Contents

PART I: LATE 1941 – LATE 1942   1

PROLOGUE   3
CHAPTER I: AN ORPHAN BOY   5
CHAPTER II: CHARLES, THE BROTHER   9
CHAPTER III: THEODORA, THE DANCER   15
CHAPTER IV: COMMODORE PERRY   21
CHAPTER V: ROSITA   31
CHAPTER VI: A THANKSGIVING SURPRISE   35
CHAPTER VII: GRACIE   43
CHAPTER VIII: LLOYD   47
CHAPTER IX: INFAMY   51
CHAPTER X: THE WAR COMES TO ORANGE GROVE   57
CHAPTER XI: THE MEETING   63
CHAPTER XII: "THE WORST DAY FOREVER"   69
CHAPTER XIII: GRACIE GOES TO WAR   73
CHAPTER XIV: NEWS FROM DES MOINES   79
CHAPTER XV: TO THE FRONT   85
CHAPTER XVI: FAREWELL, MR. SATO   93
CHAPTER XVII: THE LADY FROM VIRGINIA   99
CHAPTER XVIII: PATRICK HENRY OSBORNE   105

CHAPTER XIX: THE HOME FRONT, 1942   111
CHAPTER XX: A VISIT FROM GRACIE   115
CHAPTER XXI: A NEW DAWN   119
CHAPTER XXII: ONCE MORE UNTO THE BREACH   127
POSTSCRIPT   137

PART II: LATE 1942 – LATE 1943   139
PROLOGUE   141
CHAPTER XXIII: THE CHRISTMAS THAT WASN'T   143
CHAPTER XXIV: SCHOOL DAYS   145
CHAPTER XXV: THE MUSIC ROOM   151
CHAPTER XXVI: ETHEL COMES HOME   155
CHAPTER XXVII: THE BROWN DERBY   159
CHAPTER XXVIII: LLOYD'S ESCAPE PLAN   161
CHAPTER XXIX: THE MEMORIAL SERVICE   165
CHAPTER XXX: THE BANKA ISLAND MASSACRE   169
CHAPTER XXXI: LLOYD'S NEW ASSIGNMENT   173
CHAPTER XXXII: WILDCATTING   177
CHAPTER XXXIII: THE LAST FAMILY MEETING   181

PART III: (FRAGMENT) LATE 1943 – LATE 1944   185
CHAPTER XXXIV: RUNNING AWAY   187
CHAPTER XXXV: A NEW LIFE   191

Part I

Late 1941 – Late 1942

Prologue

Dear Reader:

This is a story of Los Angeles in the early 1940s. It is a true story, at least as I experienced it through my own eyes. I admit that I was a young child at the time the story takes place; but as I hope to make evident, my childhood was quite unusual, and I was called upon to carry out tasks well beyond my actual years. My life at the time consisted solely of observing and participating in the doings of the characters in this story, whom I will introduce to you shortly. For reasons I will explain, I was not in school during this year, nor were there any other children in my life. My entire existence revolved around these characters. My memories of this time are still vividly clear to me; but memories are very personal and malleable, are they not?

My intention is to restrict this memoir to just one year, but I think it arguable that the year in question—from late 1941 to late 1942—saw the most dramatic changes in the entire history of Los Angeles. Because of a "job" that I was given, I came to know the city very well, and the L.A. of autumn 1942 was a vastly different place than it had been just a year earlier. At the start of the 1940s, my city was in many ways a provincial town, very overgrown but still insular and small-minded. But the shock of the Japanese attack on Hawaii, and the subsequent sighting of Japanese submarines off our coastline, brought almost immediate changes in how we viewed ourselves and our city. In my own case, the constant worry over an invasion was exacerbated by the fears of many of my immediate neighbors. I lived in the Fairfax district of L.A., which was then becoming a center for the city's Jewish population. As the Nazi horrors in Europe had grown ever more ghastly, thousands of European Jews had fled; and many, especially artists, musicians and writers, had ended up in Los Angeles.

So here is my story. I hope you will find my remembrances interesting, and in some cases humorous, and that the characters in the story will intrigue and fascinate you, as they did me. However, some of my memories of early 1940s L.A. are not so happy, and a few are painfully seared in my mind even to this day.

CHAPTER I

An Orphan Boy

LOS ANGELES, NOVEMBER 1941

It was because of Mrs. O'Grady that I believed I was an orphan. Almost every morning, she would walk by my house on her way up to Pico Boulevard to shop for her day's groceries. She was a rather small woman, middle-aged, who always wore a straw hat with a flower in it. She had some kind of accent, as did many of my neighbors along Orange Grove Avenue and the next block over on Fairfax Avenue, but I was too young to figure out where in the world she might have come from. I always noticed that she was nervous, a bit fidgety, as though she was in a hurry to get somewhere; but she would never pass by my house without speaking with me. She would usually return from her shopping after an hour or so, with her little grocery cart filled with fresh vegetables, fruits and French bread. She was often accompanied on her way to or from Pico by one of her neighbors, and if so she would always stop in front of my house and say to her companion, "This is the sweet little orphan boy I was telling you about. He spends all day riding his bike around and around this courtyard." And then she would speak directly to me: "How are you today, young man?" I had been taught by my four "fathers" always to be polite, so I would answer, "I am very well, thank you." At this point Rosita, who was one of my surrogate mothers, would often emerge from her nearby doorway and greet Mrs. O'Grady, but always in Spanish. Rosita knew almost no English, but Mrs. O'Grady could speak some Spanish, and they would exchange pleasantries for a while, while I continued on my bicycle rounds.

One day I asked Rosita, "What does it mean to be an orphan?" She looked quizzically at me, and repeated, "Orphan? Orphan?" She always had her English-Spanish dictionary nearby, since no one else in our little community could speak Spanish, including her husband Homer. She had a lot of experience in looking up English words, and after a few moments she found the Spanish word for 'orphan,' and she started to laugh. She said to me, with a big smile on her face, "*Oh sí, tu eres un huérfano. Sí, no padre, no madre, un huérfano*," and she laughed even harder. From then on, Rosita would call me "the orphan boy" or *"el huérfano,"* always with a big smile on her face and a humorous lilt in her voice. It was because Rosita got so much pleasure from calling me an orphan that I thought that being one must be a really wonderful and joyous thing.

What I thought of as "my house" was actually a two-story U-shaped Spanish Mission-style building, divided into four apartments of approximately the same size, very typical of 1930s Los Angeles. The arms of the U faced out onto Orange Grove, just a block south of Pico. Apartment 1, nearest the street, was occupied by Rosita and Homer, who constituted one set of my surrogate parents. Rosita, who was Cuban, never had any problem making herself understood, since she "spoke" with her hands, body, feet and facial expressions. As far as I could tell, Homer existed solely to worship Rosita. Apartment 2, in the back of the U, was occupied by another set of my surrogate parents, Commie and Mary Margaret, who were actually my godparents (Mary Margaret was my grandmother's best friend). Apartment 3's residents were Charles, another surrogate father to me, his wife Theodora, a dancer and sometime actress, and Theodora's very elderly mother, Frances. I lived in Apartment 4, across from Apartment 1 and facing the street, with my grandparents, Grace and Patrick Henry Osborne.

A cement pathway circled the interior of the U, connecting the doorways of all four apartments. Inside the pathway was a luxuriant garden containing large ferns and various flowering plants, including birds of paradise and orchids. This pathway was my home during most of the daytime hours. I was allowed to ride my bicycle (which still had training wheels, much to my embarrassment) around and around the circle, as long as I didn't go out onto the sidewalk at Orange Grove. My riding on the pathway enabled my various surrogate parents to keep an eye on me, and whenever I was hungry or needed to go to the bathroom, I could stop in one of the apartments.

To me, the inhabitants of our little community were my family, since all nine adults took at least some part in caring for me, and in telling me about the world I was about to enter. Since I had no siblings and there were no other children in our complex, virtually all my interactions were with the adults. Except for Grace and Patrick Henry, all the other couples wanted to have children but were still childless, so I was in a sense everyone's substitute child. Grace and Patrick Henry's two adult children, one of whom was my own mother, were now far away, so my grandmother considered herself my substitute mother. It was only much later that I came to realize how disparate the members of my family were. In some ways they comprised a unique representation of Los Angeles in the early 1940s: a classic Southern California real estate developer, a movie starlet, an alcoholic, a "Latina bombshell," a faded Southern belle, and a future war hero. The shattering events of the next few months would test each person, with some very unexpected outcomes. Some people would exhibit extraordinary bravery, but others would experience tragedy and personal disaster.

What Rosita knew when she laughingly called me *"un huerfano"* was that I was not really an orphan in the usual sense of that word. I did in fact have both a living mother and father, but for reasons I will later explain, my mother could not be part of my life during this difficult time, as she lived far away. My father would remain unknown to me until many years had transpired and I had become a young man. However, for me, the warmth and security of my four families at Orange Grove was wonderful and fulfilling, which is why I accepted Mrs. Grady's description of me as a positive and happy thing.

One particular day when I was riding around my circle, I noticed that Mrs. O'Grady was standing on the sidewalk, watching me. I rode over to where she was standing. She said to me, "They had some freshly baked cookies today up at Ralph's, and they're still warm. I don't think it would hurt for you to have one." I gladly took the cookie and thanked her, and she patted me on the head. I noticed she looked at me with a special fondness, perhaps remembering some happy time with small children in her own life. She lingered a bit, and I noticed that her usual fidgety demeanor had been replaced by an expression that I could not describe, except to say that I felt a sudden sadness in my heart. I would remember that moment in future weeks when Mrs. O'Grady passed by, and I especially remembered it on the day, not long thereafter, when I would see Mrs. O'Grady for the very last time, and she would tearfully tell me a terrible secret that I can recall in perfect detail to this very day.

CHAPTER II

Charles, the Brother

One day Charles said to me, "I always wanted a son. My brother Bill has a son, and he told me it's the greatest thing in his life. But to me, you're just like my own son, and as long as I'm alive, you'll never be without a father." This impressed me very much, since I had never known my own biological father.

Charles always spoke to me as though I were an adult. He considered it his primary responsibility as a father to teach me grooming, dressing properly, and "gentlemanly" behavior. Charles would frequently say things like, "You know, son, I was raised in New York City, where people dress properly. It's very upsetting to me that many men here in Los Angeles often don't wear ties. My brother and I always wear ties, as men should." In fact, Charles was himself a very elegant man, with movie-star good looks; he always sported a perfectly trimmed moustache, and was known for his very impressive wardrobe, consisting of dark grey suits, matching vests and beautiful ties; sometimes he even wore grey fawnskin gloves. But Charles' specialty was shoes, which were always shined to a bright glow. He had black, grey, brown and two-toned shoes, depending on the color and shade of the suit he was wearing. In another age, Charles would have been known as a "dandy."

As far as I knew, my grandmother had never actually purchased any new clothes for me, preferring rather to dress me in hand-me-downs given to her by fellow employees at the May Company department store up on Wilshire. I know that some of these clothes were made for girls, but my grandmother—who was perhaps the most frugal person ever to have lived on earth—would tell me, "Girls' clothes are just as good as boys' clothes, and actually they're better, because girls don't wear them out as fast." But at some point when I was about four, Charles had thrown up his hands when he saw me wearing a frilly pink outfit, and had told my grandmother that he would henceforth take responsibility for "dressing me like a young man should be dressed." This was in fact the only task that Charles ever assumed, either on behalf of his own little family (Theodora and Frances), or for the larger community of our four families, an activity he considered a sort of God-given and sacred responsibility. Now, as I was approaching my fifth birthday, I went through a sustained growth spurt, and the outfits Charles had recently purchased for me were quickly outgrown. Charles would pretend exasperation at my growth and say things like, "I think you're going to be a giant," but he actually loved having the excuse to buy me a new wardrobe, each time selecting different colors and styles of suits and vests and pants. Each day, when he was in a "Good Charles" mode, he would make sure that all my buttons were secured and my tie properly tied, and my shoes shined to a mirror finish. At this point, Charles would step back, look at me appraisingly, and say, "You know, you're just like a son to me."

Charles' life consisted of three phases. First was the "Good Charles" times, when he would be beautifully dressed, could converse intelligently about many subjects, especially the arts, and could charm anyone. Then there was what my grandmother called the "Downfall," when he would suddenly disappear for several days and be uncontactable, existing in what Commie called "a bad place, sort of like Hell." After that was "Recovery," when he returned to his apartment and would sleep for three or four days nonstop.

Because I spent my life observing the comings and goings of my little family, Charles' routine became very familiar to me. At the onset of a "good" phase, Charles would emerge from Apartment 3 into the bright Los Angeles sunlight, blink a few times, and track me down. He would then be an attentive father, guide and educator. These periods would last a week or sometimes two, and everyone in our little community would encourage us. But inevitably, Charles' behavior would start to change in subtle but to me noticeable ways, and soon thereafter he would say something like, "I just remembered, I have an appointment up at the studio." He would then call a cab and that would be the last I would see of him for the duration of his "Downfall." My grandmother would say to me, "Well, Charles has fallen off the wagon again. Don't worry, he'll be back before too long."

As I was often outside in the courtyard, I frequently witnessed the very end of a Downfall, when a taxi would pull up in front of our apartment complex and disgorge Charles, who needed the assistance of the disgusted driver to get out of the rear seat and onto the sidewalk. His clothing was always filthy, stained and torn, his usually perfectly coiffed hair awry. He obviously hadn't shaved for days, and he invariably smelled terrible. Most times it was all he could do to stagger over to the door of Apartment 3, and on at least a few occasions in my memory, he actually crawled on hands and knees from the curb to the entryway of his apartment. I felt I should not get close to Charles when he returned from one of his downfalls, and we never spoke. He would disappear into his apartment, and no one would see him again for another several days, until he would suddenly reappear, once again the dapper New York man-about-town.

During his "Good Charles" times, he would spend a lot of time with me. He seemed to have endless stories about movie stars and different films, and even ideas about how he could have improved this or that production. Charles was the younger brother of one of the major Hollywood directors of the 1930s and '40s, William A. Seiter. Charles' brother had directed more than 50 films for studios like Universal and 20th Century Fox, and had directed stars like Fred Astaire, Ginger Rogers, Henry Fonda, Shirley Temple and John Wayne. Although William Seiter had directed all kinds of films over the years, his highest rated and most critically praised films were musicals and comedies. In fact, he directed what is still considered one of the greatest comedies of all time, *Sons of the Desert*, starring Stan Laurel and Oliver Hardy at the peak of their popularity. William had taken his brother Charles to many studio parties and knew most of the great stars of the time. People often said that William and Charles looked like twins, since both were very tall, slender, aristocratic looking, and elegantly dressed.

William Seiter had been one of the foremost pioneers of early Hollywood. He had come out west from New York in 1912 and had played in very early silent movies as a bit actor and stuntman, at the famous Keystone Studios. By 1915, he was both acting in and directing silent films, and quickly became known as a workaholic who could get films done quickly and cheaply. In 1919 alone, he directed nine films for the National Film Corporation. At the peak of his success in the late 1930s, it was said that he was a favorite director of several major studios like Universal and 20th Century Fox, because he knew how to sweet-talk his often difficult stars into cooperating to get a film done on time and under budget.

In 1920, William sent for his brother Charles, in the hopes of including him in the rapidly growing movie industry, but unfortunately Charles was already showing signs of a certain instability, and within a few years of arriving in Los Angeles he had become a serious drinker. In the early days of Hollywood, alcoholism was by no means a rare condition among actors, screenwriters, musicians and others in the business, but many were able to still do their jobs while semi-drunk or hungover. Charles, however, was not among these, and he became unreliable and too often unemployable, since once he started drinking he couldn't stop, and would soon lose all control of himself.

Perhaps because William took personal blame for bringing his brother out to Hollywood, he also accepted responsibility for Charles' life and well-being. He would frequently come by Orange Grove to check up on how Charles was doing. On those favorable occasions when Charles was sober, the two would hug and laugh and talk about home and family back in New York. Charles called his brother "Bill" or "Billy," although interestingly, William never called Charles "Chuck" or "Charlie," but always Charles.

Most of the members of my little family were in awe of William, who was always referred to as "Mr. Seiter," except of course by Charles. Mr. Seiter's arrival always caused a bit of a flurry in my neighborhood of modest houses, with his long black limousine pulling up in front of our apartment building. A liveried driver would hop out and scurry around to open the rear door for Mr. Seiter, who would emerge dressed in elegant clothing, often accompanied by a star or two from the film he was currently directing. (Mr. Seiter once told me that when he needed to work with one of his actors on their roles, having them ride around town in the back of his limousine was a perfect way to get them alone. I clearly remember one day when both Fred Astaire and Rita Hayworth were with him.)

It often happened that I was somewhere around my bicycle circle when Mr. Seiter's limousine pulled up, and I would pedal quickly to be near the street when he emerged. He would say to me, "Gary, how are you this fine day? Do you by any chance know where my brother is?" I did in fact always know where he was, but if he was in a Downfall, I would say, "I think he's gone away for a few days, Mr. Seiter," and Charles' brother's face would fall, and he would suddenly look old and unhappy. At this point, Mr. Seiter would sometimes sit down on the little concrete wall that separated our garden from my path and put his face in his hands. Once he said to me, "I wish we could cure Charles' problem—if we could do that, I could give him a wonderful job, and then he could be a real full-time father to you. He would love that, and so would you and so would I. Charles knows how much I love my own son. I'd happily give up everything I have for him." Then Mr. Seiter would say, "Gary, do you know that my own son, Christopher, is only a few years older than you? If only Charles could experience having his own son…" and his voice would trail off. Sometimes the two of us would just sit, not speaking, but both perhaps thinking the same thoughts.

CHAPTER III

Theodora, the Dancer

Charles' wife was Theodora, known to all of us simply as Ted. They had met on a movie set a few years before. Both were tall, slim and very attractive, but both had serious demons. Charles' was alcohol, but Ted's was harder to explain. She was very emotional and tempestuous, given to fits of rage that she released by screaming and sometimes throwing things. It was obvious that Charles was seriously afraid of Ted, and when she would fly into a rage, he would quickly leave their apartment, sometimes even hiding among the tall and overgrown bird of paradise plants in the middle of our shared garden. Sometimes, as I made my rounds, I would see cigar smoke coming from the interior of our garden, and I knew that Charles was in there somewhere.

Ted always described herself to me as an "actress." In retrospect, I think a more fitting description would have been "chorus girl" or "showgirl." I do know that she had once been very good friends with Rita Hayworth, and that the two of them had been dancers in Tijuana, Mexico, during the Prohibition years, when thousands of Californians crossed the border on weekends to drink legally, gamble, and attend shows. Ted and Rita had remained friends long after their Tijuana dancing days were over, and Ted had many pictures of herself with "Rita Cansino" (Rita Hayworth's stage name when she was a dancer, "Cansino" having been her birth name). Ted and Rita still hung out at times, perhaps drawn together by their scandalous pasts and the demons that both confronted on a daily basis.

A few times Charles took me to see Ted dance. In those days, at the still-surviving grand movie palaces, the usual practice was to have a movie double feature, a newsreel, a cartoon, plus a live vaudeville-type show, with live dancers and singers and sometimes a magician. Although it was an exciting experience, when I actually saw the show live, I was unable to make out Ted from the ten or so other chorus girls, all of whom were of similar height and wore identical costumes.

It was my grandmother's belief that Ted had been one of the dancers in the great Busby Berkeley films of the 1930s, many of which featured two dozen or more dancing girls dressed in wild, often risqué costumes, before the imposition of the censorious "Code" in 1934. Unfortunately, none of the dancing girls in the Berkeley or similar films were ever credited, so no one can say for sure in which films Ted appeared. Even today, 70 years later, I still look for her visage in the great musical films of the 1930s, but so far without success.

When I spoke to Ted, I always called her "Aunt Ted," since she was in fact one of my very few blood relatives. Ted's mother Frances, or "Aunt Fan" as I knew her, was my grandfather's sister. To say the least, Ted stood out in the Osborne family. She was tall, while the other Osbornes were tiny. She was glamorous, while the rest of the family was somewhat homely. She was brash and outgoing and loud, while the rest of the Osbornes were conservative and quiet and humble. She dressed in garish colors, wore bright red lipstick, and allowed a fair amount of cleavage to show, while the other Osborne women dressed as conservatively and unobtrusively as possible. Clearly my grandmother, the strongest personality in our family by far, did not approve of Ted or her demeanor, and Ted returned her disapproval with an air of dismissal. But as Commie told me, I was the lucky one, because Ted, childless then and forever, treated me as her substitute son.

When Ted was home—which was not that often—she would always seek me out, and sometimes took me to meet her fellow dancers or the stars of the films she was working on. In later years, I realized she was probably allowed on the set of any film that her brother-in-law William Seiter was directing, including ones starring John Wayne, Abbott and Costello, Fred Astaire or Shirley Temple. Sometimes Ted was gone for weeks at a time; she would imply that she was off working on a movie, but the details were often vague, and I can find no record of her being credited for an acting role for any movie filmed on location.

Ted's birth name had been Theodora Mitchell. Her father had supposedly been a wealthy attorney in San Francisco. I never learned how Ted's mother and father met, or what had happened to their marriage. All I knew, as seen through my grandmother's somewhat skeptical eyes, was that the marriage had not lasted very long, and that Ted was Frances' only child and took after her father.

From what I heard, Ted danced or acted under different names. When she was in Tijuana dancing with Rita Cansino, she was known as "Conchita Mitchell." When she and Charles were part of my family living on Orange Grove, she was "Conchita Seiter," or "Ted Osborne." Ted had a huge stack of glossy 8 x 10 publicity photos, most of which showed her in Busby Berkeley-style costumes, each more outlandish than the last. When she was home, she would often say, "Gary, come and see my latest photo shoot—this is from my current job," and she would show me her newest publicity shots. For me, this was a door into a world I could not even imagine being part of, and I loved hearing "Conchita" tell me stories of the sets and the locations, the productions she was part of. I wish I still had a copy of one of Ted's glossy publicity photos, but they are all lost in the dust of time.

When Ted was home, there was a decent chance that Charles was off on a binge or in bed recovering, so they weren't often seen together as a couple. Occasionally, however, Charles and Ted would appear together in love and harmony, Charles in one of his exquisite suits and Ted in one of her flattering gowns, and the two of them would go out for dinner at Chasen's or the Brown Derby or another of Hollywood's luxury restaurants. A few times they took me along as sort of their faux son, and I got to experience a style of life that I would never forget. On those occasions, Charles would indulge in his favorite activity of dressing me up like a life-sized doll, and Ted delighted in adding some little flourish, such as a flower for my coat lapel. But even at my young age, I could detect a sadness in both of their eyes at the end of such evenings, when they had to return me to the reality of our Orange Grove complex.

Ted once told me that when she was a little girl she had a horse, and had always felt very comfortable riding and taking care of them. Ted had become acquainted with the famous director John Ford, and eventually Ted became his official wrangler, in charge of the horses which appeared in his movies. Ted sometimes took me to parties where Ford's latest film was being shot, and when we arrived, Ted would quickly introduce me to the players, who might include Joanne Dru, Ward Bond, Robert Mitchum or John Wayne, whom I clearly remember meeting. Ted would proudly describe me as "her boy," but after the introductions I would be exiled to a sort of children's village, where the kids of cast members and technicians were taken care of while the adults drank and caroused. The Ford ranch had a very big swimming pool, which we children were allowed to use, and that is actually where I learned how to swim.

In the terrors and tribulations that were awaiting our little family, Ted would share fully in our family's torments. Yet, ironically, the routine of her own life would change very little. It has been said that "show business" goes on, no matter what is happening in the outside world. Ted would prove that old canard to be eerily true.

CHAPTER IV

Commodore Perry

It was Commie who gave me my first real "job." I became his "associate," but in fact I was sort of a very youthful con man. It was Commie who discovered the commercial potential of what Charles was working so hard to create in me, namely a youthful exemplar of class and sophistication.

Commie was extremely proud of his true name—Commodore Perry Averett—and would tell the story of how the man for whom he had been named, U.S. Navy Commodore Matthew Perry, had, through the force of his will and the power of his personality, singlehandedly "opened" Japan to the West via his famous voyage into Tokyo Bay in the 1850s. Commie loved all things Navy-related: sailing ships, modern warships, Navy garb, storms at sea and famous battles. Commie got to tell his stories almost every day, because he was a prototypical Southern California real estate man, and was almost always trying to sell something to somebody.

Commie both envied Charles and sympathized with him. In fact Commie, who was only of medium height with a rather stocky build, often told Charles that he wished he was as tall and distinguished looking as he was, but Commie did his best to keep up with Charles in the sartorial realm. When Charles was sober, the two of them spent a lot of time together, and sometimes included me in their conversations. Both were married to "difficult" women, both were childless despite their strong desires to have children, and both had dreams that were as yet unfulfilled. Since they occupied the two adjacent rear apartments, and since both their wives were usually absent during the day, they could engage in "guy talk" with each other. I was often the subject of their conversations, since Commie agreed with Charles' desire to turn me into a "young gentleman." I recall one conversation involving the three of us, where the two decided they needed to plan carefully for my future for the next 15 years, including where I would go to college. Charles said that I should definitely go to school in New York, since he felt that was the only way I could wash off the provinciality of my Los Angeles upbringing. Commie, who was unquestionably an enthusiastic "L.A. Booster," argued for somewhere nearer home, so that I "wouldn't entirely forget my southern and western roots."

Of all the people in our little community, Commie had the most sympathy for Charles' periodic downfalls. Many times Commie would say to Charles and me, "Don't worry, Charles, if you need to go away for a while, I'll take good care of Gary here," and in fact he would devote extra time to me while Charles was, as he put it, "in Hell."

Next to the Navy, what Commie loved best was buying or leasing vacant land or farmland, and building houses on it. Commie was thus part of the great tradition of Los Angeles real estate entrepreneurs and developers dating back to the nineteenth century, including such people as Edward Mulholland and Henry Huntington. Commie would arrange all the financing for his projects, and for installation of electricity, sewage, and access to water and other infrastructure, and would then work with school boards to plan for new schools. He would hire architects and builders and would start constructing his houses. When the first houses in his subdivision had been finished, Commie would move on to his favorite part of the process—the actual selling of individual houses and apartment complexes. To Commie, everything about what he called "the Southland"—by which he meant the Los Angeles Basin and the San Fernando Valley—was wonderful, spacious, and subject to his own brand of salesmanship.

One morning I happened to be wearing an elegant new ensemble that Charles had bought for me. As usual, I was making my bicycle rounds around our complex. Commie came out of his apartment doorway, dressed as he always was in a checkered sport coat with dark blue trousers, a Scottish plaid vest, and bright tie. When he saw me, he started to say what he typically said when he was heading off to do some real estate dealings, such as "Gary, you be sure to check in with Rosita every 15 minutes or so." But this time he stopped in mid-sentence, and suddenly looked very closely at me in an appraising manner. After a moment of contemplation, he said, "Gary, how would you like to go along with me today and see what I do?" I always liked my time with Commie, and I told him that I would enjoy going with him very much. Commie quickly went over to Rosita's door and let her know, and then we were off.

Commie owned the biggest and fanciest car of anyone in our complex, a beautiful cream-colored Packard, one of the most desirable cars of its time. I knew that the car was part of Commie's overall image as a big-time developer. We climbed into the spacious interior, and he drove up to Pico, turned left, and headed over to Sepulveda, which was the main highway from Los Angeles proper northward to the San Fernando Valley. While we were driving north, Commie started explaining to me what he would be doing. "This development is a pretty small one, only about 200 houses. I tried to expand it, but the city's building a reservoir along the north end. The first ten houses are ready to sell, and today I have some clients, so we'll get the process started. Once I sell the first ten, the others will go like hotcakes. I'm anxious to do my next development project, which will be down around Hawthorne. That'll be a big one." I actually understood very little of what Commie was saying, but it all sounded exciting and complicated, and I thought to myself I would learn as much as I could.

When we came down Sepulveda into the Valley, Commie pointed out various neighborhoods such as Sherman Oaks and Encino, and told me who had developed them, when they were built, and how each had been incorporated into the ever-expanding city limits of Los Angeles. After a few minutes, Commie turned his Packard off the main highway and onto what looked like a country lane, and soon we arrived at a construction site, with many workers building houses and bulldozers moving dirt around to create new sites. At the entrance to the development was a very large sign featuring a drawing of a lovely new house, with the words: "Buy now, best prices, best selection." Commie drove by the sign, and just inside the construction area were several newly built houses that, unlike the rest, were painted and had lawns and foliage, and a paved street in front. Commie told me, "We always finish a few houses first and get them furnished and landscaped, so we can start selling as soon as possible. Ah, I see my clients over there...just come along with me, but don't say anything," at which point he pulled up in front of the "sample home."

Commie and I got out of his car, and I followed him to where his clients were waiting. They were a casually dressed, attractive young couple. Commie greeted them with a hail-fellow-well-met tone in his voice, and said, "You must be Mr. Robinson! And this is Mrs. Robinson? So very happy to meet you, and I want to thank you for taking time to visit this wonderful new development." I was unsure of where I should be standing, so I positioned myself somewhat behind and to the side of Commie. Just as he was ready to launch into his standard sales pitch, the young woman said, "And who might this young man be?" For just the briefest moment I could tell that Commie was unsure what to say, but then in the next instant, we both saw the same thing. It was as if we had both been hit by a lightning bolt from Zeus! It was in her eyes. She wanted this house, and she wanted this brand-new community, but most of all, she wanted someone like me, a fine, upstanding, well-dressed young gentleman of a son. She was young and newly married and wanted a lovely new house, a community to belong to, and her own family. The warm glow in her eyes said it all. And in that brief moment was born my new role: I would be the image of the future that Commie would use over and over again, to convince potential buyers that this was their time to buy into the Southland Dream.

Mr. and Mrs. Robinson were typical of thousands of others in Los Angeles at that time: newlyweds (or about to be), fresh in from Iowa or Wisconsin or Ohio, already with a good job in the booming defense industry companies that had made Los Angeles the national leader in aircraft manufacture and weapons production. Many of the men like Mr. Robinson had secured jobs in engineering or other technical roles with North American Aviation or Douglas or Lockheed. They were not blue-collar workers but college graduates, or had at least attended some college in the Midwest. The Mr. Robinsons were thinking about their new jobs, what kind of car to buy, and where the next "settlers' picnic" would be. (The *Los Angeles Times* would often have notices that said things like, "All folks from Missouri, be sure to attend this weekend's gala picnic at Exposition Park, featuring KC burgers.") But more important to Commie, the Mrs. Robinsons were thinking, now that they had arrived in the

Southland Paradise, it was time to buy a nice house in a nice community with nice people, and start their families.

I think Commie and I both sensed that Mrs. Robinson was ready to tell her husband that 'this is the place.' Commie just needed to seal the deal. He said, "Mrs. Robinson, I'm so pleased that you noticed Gary here. Today is the first day he's accompanying me in my work, and I wanted him to see the very first house in this brand-new part of the beautiful San Fernando Valley. I would like for you, Mr. and Mrs. Robinson, to meet this outstanding young man. I am proud to say that he is my godson, and he represents the future of our great city and our great region." Commie was hitting his stride, and the words flowed. "The Southland is the best place in the entire world to live and raise a family. Did you know that many of the greatest minds in the world, novelists and philosophers and musicians and composers, have just moved into our great city? Yes, my friends, our future couldn't be brighter. My godson here"—at this point Commie nudged me forward so he could point to me, pat me on the head, and maintain eye contact with his clients all at the same time—"is the first generation to be born here, to be raised here, and to spend their productive lives here. There is nowhere on earth that has a future like the Southland. And you, my friends, can be part of…our family." When Commie said the words "our family," there was a little catch in his throat, as though the thought of our beautiful future together was so overwhelming that his emotions were about to get the better of him. Commie now had his clients, especially Mrs. Robinson, in the palm of his hand. He said, "Please come with me to see this truly beautiful new house, just completed, and the first of more than 200 that will make up this wonderful neighborhood." I could tell that Commie was now sure of the sale.

From then on, Commie always tried very hard to get his prospective buyers to bring along their wives, explaining that there might be certain issues, such as paint colors or garden styles, "that the missus would have a special interest in." Commie's potential buyers did in fact usually bring their wives (or fiancées or girlfriends), and my presence pretty much assured Commie of a quick sale at a top price. The "join our family" words, with a catch in his throat, and Commie's introduction of me as his godson, were always emotional, and Commie would give me a special hug of pride and affection that was beyond what any woman could resist. At just the right moment, Commie would produce, from an inside pocket of his suit jacket, a contract document, which he would explain did not commit the client to any "permanent" arrangement (when in fact it did), but was just to "hold the property" since it was in such great demand.

Selling individual houses was like picking low-hanging fruit for Commie, especially when he had me as his willing and emotion-producing accomplice. What Commie really wanted was to be "a famous developer," with subdivisions as well-known as Reseda or Tarzana or Hyde Park. The closest he came was with Mar Vista, a development in L.A.'s Westside near the Pacific Ocean, which Commie claimed as his own creation. Commie sometimes took me along to his Mar Vista meetings, and I remember coming home with my shoes full of sand, since the land on which Mar Vista was developed consisted of sand dunes. In retrospect I think most of the houses in Commie's Mar Vista development were literally built on sand. In recent years I have thought about going back to Los Angeles to see where all of Commie's houses have ended up, given the well-known peregrinations of sand dunes; but I have resisted that impulse, preferring to keep intact my memory of Commie proudly using me as the symbol of the "Southland of the Future."

Of all my mothers and fathers, Commie was the only one who would in a sense prosper from the catastrophic events about to befall us all. Indeed, his remarkable salesmanship skills would be put to new and unexpected uses in the weeks ahead. The two great disappointments in Commie's life—that he had never actually served in the Navy, and that he and Mary Margaret had been unable to produce any children—would be at least partly overcome by his new role in the weeks ahead, and by his increasing feeling that I was "almost his own son."

Commie's wife Mary Margaret was a pretty but unremarkable woman, starting to enter middle age. Because she was a first-grade teacher, she was more familiar with the needs and desires of a boy my age than my other caregivers. She was my grandmother's best friend, and they both had early work schedules—my grandmother as a May Company sales clerk who worked the morning shift, and Mary Margaret as a school teacher. Often my grandmother would work a double shift at the May Company, but when she got home early she would go over to Mary Margaret's apartment, so they could commiserate about problems with their spouses or work issues, or the general lowly state of the world. I was sometimes privy to these conversations if there was no other caregiver available; my grandmother would give me some toys to play with or a book to read, and she and Mary Margaret would then proceed to talk about some very personal and intimate matters, presumably assuming that this child had no inkling what they were talking about. I think they underestimated what I could comprehend about sex and unfaithfulness, and I did understand at least the gist of what they were complaining about, especially when it came to relations with their husbands, which apparently had cooled considerably in recent years.

Ironically, although Mary Margaret was the least memorable of the nine men and women in my young life, she was the one who stayed in my life the longest, indeed until my eventual departure from California in the 1960s. She remained my grandmother's friend, confidante, and ultimately her fellow rebel and drama queen, and the two of them became, unexpectedly, rather wild and woolly ladies in later life. But before they reached that stage of life, they would both have immense chasms to cross; and for one of them, the abyss was only a few short months away.

CHAPTER V

Rosita

Of the four women who were my mother-substitute caregivers, only Rosita was home most of the time, since my grandmother and Mary Margaret and Ted all worked very long hours outside our home. When Charles and Commie were not available to look after me, it was usually Rosita who would step in. I knew that Rosita had always wanted to have her own children; so, as with Charles and Commie, I became a substitute child for her. Rosita was Cuban and flamboyantly Latina: she always wore a red or pink flower in her hair, dressed in bright gaudy colors, wore cherry red lipstick and lots of makeup and was permanently surrounded by a penumbra of perfume that followed her everywhere. Rosita was always in one extreme mood or another—mostly joyfulness, but sometimes anger or outrage. Rosita personified the Latina female of 1930s movies, and when Charles' brother would visit us, Rosita always made him laugh, I think because she reminded him of some of the famous Latina "bombshells" he had directed in recent years. In fact, Mr. Seiter himself had been married to the famously mercurial Laura LaPlante some years earlier, so perhaps Rosita reminded him of his younger and wilder days.

Rosita was a wonderful mother to me, easily the most affectionate and passionate of the four women, always concerned over any little injury I might have suffered from a fall off my bicycle. I quickly learned that any small scrape, feigned or not, could result in extended periods of Rosita's fussing and kissing and general attention, which for a boy of my young age was like manna from heaven. I loved that Rosita was totally unlike Mary Margaret or Ted or my grandmother in style, attitude, and approach to life.

In later years I came to assume that Rosita's colorful and passionate personality was a product of her self-creation, based on watching Lupe Vélez ("the Mexican Spitfire") in many films. Rosita was also the only creative and active cook among my four families. Her apartment always smelled rich, aromatic and inviting. At my young age I knew nothing of spices and different styles of cooking, but I did know that Rosita and Homer's apartment was a different world, and one that I loved. Whenever Rosita was cooking a meal, which was most of the time, I wanted to be in her kitchen just to absorb the smells and to see her feverishly filling skillets with unknown ingredients, chattering away all the while in Spanish to no one in particular, letting me taste dishes that were exotic and strange but so exciting to me.

Rosita always spoke Spanish, to me and to everyone else. I seldom understood the meaning of her actual words, but I could often intuit the content of what she was saying. It helped that Rosita never stopped talking. If it was important that she convey a specific fact to me, she would consult her beaten-up leather-bound Spanish-English dictionary and say something like, "Gary, *es muy importante...a las* eleven o'clock...Commie..."—pausing to look up a word—"...pick you up."

When the crises of the near future befell us all, the protectiveness Rosita had always exhibited toward me would intensify, and there were times when the only place I could find solace and peace was with her. I believe those times were essential to my mental health and stability. Many years later I was able to visit Cuba in person, and the smells and tastes of Cuban cooking returned me to the happy times in Rosita's kitchen.

Rosita's husband Homer was the personification of Middle America; I believe he was from Oklahoma or Kansas. He was a rather small and thin man, of average looks, and now well into middle age. He worked in an upscale men's shoe store up on Wilshire Boulevard, often six days a week. Homer's main contribution to my life was that he had had the good sense to marry Rosita and that he was a kind and loving husband. He always seemed bemused by Rosita's antics and performances, but seemed aware that he could never outshine her and so never tried. He was like the canvas on which Rosita's brilliant colors had been painted, and he was content with that. I never knew how Homer had met Rosita, although my grandmother once told me he had met her in Cuba while he was with the U.S. Army during the occupation of Cuba.

Once home from work, Homer would say little, settling into an easy chair in his living room and floating through the evening, happily absorbing the aromas, sounds, flowers and colors of his wife's creations. Several times a week Homer and Rosita would play bridge with Commie and Mary Margaret. Homer had worked out a scheme whereby Rosita would almost always be "dummy," since she didn't really enjoy playing, preferring instead to be flitting about, bringing drinks and snacks, and perhaps arranging flowers. Of all my "fathers," Homer was the least competitive and most relaxed, a quality I came to envy in later life. However, Homer's life was also about to change, and he began to emerge from the shadow cast by Rosita's powerful character.

CHAPTER VI

A Thanksgiving Surprise

It was the greatest party of my life. All four of my families were there, even Ted and her mother Fan, along with some people I did not know who I assumed were neighbors. The party was held in Rosita's apartment, since her kitchen was best equipped to prepare and serve large amounts of food. Although Rosita's dining table could only seat eight people, other families brought folding bridge tables, which, arranged in a makeshift pattern, brought us all together. Each family brought a characteristic dish: Rosita had prepared Cuban beans and rice, and a sausage platter; my grandmother had baked several "Virginia-style" pumpkin pies as well as a spicy mincemeat pie; Mary Margaret made her famous waffles; and Aunt Fan delivered "food from our own country," by which she meant the Confederacy, consisting of sweet potatoes, rich buttery biscuits and mustard greens. The turkey was the biggest I had ever seen, and Rosita had somehow managed to stuff it into her oven, where it had roasted for many hours. The smell of the roasting turkey and all the other dishes was, to me, overwhelming.

I was especially happy that Charles was in a "Good Charles" phase—he added a certain elegance to our little group, and he seemed to be getting along with Ted for a change. I knew from my careful observations that he and Ted were often fighting or arguing about something. It was obvious to me that Ted considered Charles to be a colossal failure, especially when compared to his brother, but on this occasion they seemed to be happy together, and were actually holding hands. Indeed, they were by far the most elegant-looking couple at the dinner, and the aura of their happiness somehow transformed the rest of us.

After everyone had eaten to their fullest, Commie stood up to address our assembly. Commie loved to take charge of such occasions and usually would make a little speech, and for this Thanksgiving he was in rare form: "First, let us once again give thanks to the Lord for all this food we have consumed." (Commie had also said a rather lengthy and complicated grace, involving several Biblical quotes, before the meal.) "We have today assembled the most unusual and wonderful group of families and guests. Over here"—pointing to my grandfather—"is the famous patriot Patrick Henry!" At this point, everyone except me laughed heartily, because they understood that Commie was going beyond even his usual level of exaggeration, into parody and satire. I did not laugh, because at my young age I took whatever Commie said as gospel truth. "And over here is our beloved friend Charles Seiter, and his lovely wife, Theodora, who we're sure will star in one of Charles' brother's great movies very soon." Both Charles and Ted stood up to take a theatrical and grandiose bow. "And, of course, we all love Theodora's mother, Frances, whom we know to be one of the great experts on American history." Commie articulated the word "American" in a particular way, so we understood that he was referring to Fan's conception of America, namely Virginia and Virginians, from Washington and Jefferson to Lee. Finally Commie said, "And thank you especially to our lovely and vivacious hostess, Rosita, and her fine upstanding husband Homer," at which point Rosita did a little dance around the room, encouraging the laughter and applause of all our families.

The part of the evening that I remember most vividly came next: Commie had introduced everyone at the table except me, and I was thinking he was going to pass over me since I was just a child, but then he said, "There is one young man here who I have not yet introduced, and he is certainly the best gentleman among us, and undoubtedly destined for great things. I am referring, of course, to Mr. Gary Anthony Glenn." At this point everyone stood up and applauded, and then the group sang "For He's a Jolly Good Fellow." I had never heard this song before, and I didn't yet know what "destined" meant, but I certainly understood what applause meant, and I believe I was too embarrassed to say anything other than "thank you." A few years later I might have given a little speech, but at that young age, such adulation was overwhelming. I understood that Commie exaggerated everything, and that he was a showman, but this was the first time that I had ever been the center of attention of such a large group of people, not just my own family but neighbors and strangers as well. I never forgot that moment.

Just as we were finishing dinner, something unexpected happened. There was a knock on Rosita's front door, and when she answered, there was Charles' brother William standing in the doorway. He was accompanied by a very beautiful young woman, and a child of about my own age. Before Mr. Seiter could say anything, Rosita, speaking animatedly in Spanish, grabbed Mr. Seiter's hand and pulled him into the room. Almost everyone had met him before, and there were greetings flowing and handshakes, and of course a big hug between the brothers. Amidst the excitement, Mr. Seiter put up his hands in order to gain everyone's attention. He said to all of us, "I'm so happy to see that you all are having a wonderful Thanksgiving Day," and looking at the remains of the turkey, dressing, potatoes and pies, he continued, "and I can see that you've enjoyed a wonderful feast. I only wanted to drop by to pay my respects to my beloved brother Charles"—with whom he was already holding hands—"to his beautiful bride, Theodora, and to Charles' mother-in-law, Fan. And also, greetings to my good friend here, Gary, whom I have observed is always on guard at the entrance to your complex, and with whom I have had some very worthwhile conversations." When Mr. Seiter said this, I remember thinking that our "conversations" had usually been about Charles and his tragic situation, and that the content of our talks were unknown to the others.

Then Mr. Seiter said, "I think some of you have not yet met my most wonderful and talented wife Marian, and certainly not my son, Christopher." At this point, Mr. Seiter's wife and son, who had been standing rather shyly near the doorway, smiled and waved to our group, though without much enthusiasm. I could tell that Christopher was a little older than I was, but we were about the same height, and we were both dressed in suits, vests and ties. This was the first time I had ever laid eyes on Mr. Seiter's own son, and I immediately recognized that this was the model Mr. Seiter so badly wanted Charles to emulate. In our formal attire, Christopher and I looked remarkably similar, and I could now better understand why Mr. Seiter envisioned me as a beloved surrogate son to Charles and Theodora.

Mr. Seiter, who as a director of films was a master of taking control of situations and people, now said to all of us, "I only have a few moments to spend with you today, because Marian and I and my son are expected at a studio Thanksgiving celebration, but I would like to speak with you about a matter of the greatest importance." At this point all of us sat down, even Mr. Seiter's wife (who was in fact the famous actress Marian Nixon) and their son Christopher. Mr. Seiter, now standing in the center of the room, said in a very serious and formal tone, "I don't wish to be the bearer of bad news, but because of my position, I'm privy to certain information, and I must be honest in telling you that I believe our country is in great danger. Many of my colleagues are recent immigrants from France and Germany and Eastern Europe, and most of them still have family there, and their reports are very ominous indeed. Many people in this country do not understand what is happening right now to Jews throughout Europe, but many of the people with whom I work have recently escaped from there, and they tell of horrendous things, almost beyond belief. Of course, Charles and I are Jews, and if our father and mother had not come to this country, we would ourselves be suffering these horrors. And now we're facing a new threat from the East, namely the Empire of Japan. Circumstances may occur in the next days and weeks that will change all of our lives. Given the dangers our country now faces, I wanted you to understand that I consider you—all of you—to be my own family, and I will protect you to the extent that I can. Of course, you know that Charles here is my own flesh and blood, but the rest of you are connected to Charles, and therefore to me, by marriage or friendship, and I want you to know that I will never forsake my own family."

My impression was that none of my four families understood very well what Mr. Seiter was talking about. None of the adults were very conversant with world affairs or current events. There was something immunizing about living in Southern California—the weather was so mild and comfortable, and the lifestyle so free and casual, that the events in Warsaw or Brussels or Prague seemed to be taking place on another planet. Of course we were vaguely aware that war was once again raging in Europe, but could it really affect our lives? The images of Southern California life that had been created and sold by real estate developers in order to attract settlers from the East Coast and Midwest, and the constant proliferation of those images by the boosters in the L.A.

newspapers, had been absorbed by everyone. I think we all believed our beloved "California lifestyle" would be with us forever, and that we were somehow immune from the horrors being experienced by millions of people in Europe and Asia.

At this point, Mr. Seiter thanked each of us individually, and he and his wife and son quickly departed. Mr. Seiter's remarks had temporarily changed the atmosphere of our celebration, and we were, for a few minutes, a somber and thoughtful group, until Commie stood up and spoke to us. "I'm sure that Mr. Seiter's remarks have given all of us something to think about," he said. "But also, let's be sure to thank the Lord that all of us have enjoyed such a wonderful Thanksgiving Day. I think we should start planning right now for an equally joyous Christmas season, and for another wonderful feast on the birthday of the Lord Jesus just one month from today. And now, it looks to me like there are more than enough Thanksgiving dinner leftovers for everyone, so let's start dividing up the morsels." On that more cheerful note, our Thanksgiving Day was over.

Unbeknownst to all of us, at the very moment we were dividing up the drumsticks and stuffing and pies, a few thousand miles away one of the most powerful naval attack fleets in history was preparing for simultaneous attacks on the Philippines, Malaya, French Indochina, the Dutch East Indies, and most dramatically, the home base for the United States Navy fleet for the entire Pacific region. Within hours, a large portion of the Japanese attack force, including five ultra-modern aircraft carriers carrying 157 attack airplanes, would steam off into the frigid North Pacific Ocean towards a secret rendezvous point near the United States territory of Hawaii. Little did any of us know that many thousands of American soldiers, sailors and airmen in Hawaii and the Philippines had less than 17 days left to live. On a very personal level, a central and beloved member of our own family would be among those who would be in the gravest danger. Even as we were finishing the last remnants of our Thanksgiving dinner, all of our lives were about to be changed forever. Our complacent and comfortable "Southern California lifestyle" would soon shatter into tiny shards.

CHAPTER VII

Gracie

At the end of each workday, my grandmother Gracie would hurry home in order to review carefully what I had, or had not, accomplished during the day, and she would take charge of my life until bedtime. Gracie was a very small and thin woman, slightly graying, but very youthful in appearance, body language and attitude. I thought of my grandmother, then as now, as a tightly coiled spring, eager to wring every possible opportunity from each moment of the day and night. Even at my youthful age, I found that my grandmother tired me out with her energy, forcefulness and aspirations.

Her full name was Grace Elaine Osborne (maiden name Rybon) and she had been born in the town of Prescott, in the high country of northern Arizona, the offspring of formerly well-to-do Southerners who had left Virginia and North Carolina because of the economic depression after the Civil War. She now worked as a clerk at the huge new May Company department store, only six blocks from our apartment complex, up on Wilshire Boulevard. Gracie often worked double shifts at the store and was usually gone before I woke up in the morning, so the first face I saw when I awoke was often Rosita, waiting for me to arise so she could take me to her apartment and serve me *desayuno Cubano*." Gracie often worked a shift on Saturdays, but regardless of when she returned, she always made a point to have a little talk with me about what I had done during the day, what "lessons of life" I had learned, and whether I had done anything "useful." She was very particular that all people—children, adults and the elderly—should be sure to do something useful every day. I was never quite sure how she defined "useful," but as time went by, I did start to absorb her philosophy. For instance, if I had spent the day bicycling around the interior of our compound, I knew that Gracie would not consider that to be useful; but if I had drawn a picture of a neighborhood cat which she could paste up in our kitchen, she deemed that useful. Even more "useful" was if I had accompanied Commie on a sales visit and played my role as his ideal child. Essentially, producing anything tangible was useful, while mere exercise, or listening to stories, was not useful, and therefore in a sense wasteful.

My grandmother had a very pragmatic view of life, perhaps the result of her own upbringing on the wild Arizona frontier. In fact, my grandmother's father had been a mineworker in late nineteenth-century Arizona, which at the time was still a non-self-governing territory of the United States, decades away from becoming a legitimate state. As a mine worker, my great-grandfather had moved from place to place depending on which mine needed his work, and one of the places my grandmother had lived for several years was Tombstone. For many years I thought my grandmother must have been an eyewitness to the infamous clash of the Earps vs. the Clantons at the shootout at the O.K. Corral; although when I got to high school, a little checking in the World Almanac indicated that the gunfight had taken place a few years before she was born. Nonetheless, I do clearly recall her telling me that she had known Wyatt Earp when she was a young child, and that her own brother, Worth Rybon, had trained to be a lawman with Mr. Earp. A few years in the future, I would move temporarily with my grandmother to her hometown of Prescott, and I got to know Gracie's brother Worth, who was still serving as sheriff of Prescott. I remember him as being at least seven feet tall, and he wore a huge revolver on his hip. He had a reputation for keeping the peace in Prescott, with his fists if necessary, on Saturday nights when the cowboys would come to town from neighboring ranches to drink and carouse.

The calamitous events that were about to happen would affect Gracie more than anyone else in my family, and her life would change in profound and unexpected ways. Within a short time, she would take on a new and extremely dramatic role.

CHAPTER VIII

Lloyd

In the early years of my life, my mother's brother Lloyd was like my older brother, who took me on adventures and taught me how to scurry near the boundaries of what was acceptable behavior. At times he was like the father I never had, who would prevent me from doing dangerous things, and would teach me "proper" behavior, or at least how to fake propriety. At other times Lloyd was like a playmate, who would engage in games with me or take me to the beach. Lloyd could also be a more senior uncle, an adviser, or a sympathetic confidant. Best of all, Lloyd had a mischievous, rebellious character, very unlike the other Osbornes. He introduced me to things that my grandmother would have been dismayed to discover. Lloyd's central motto was that life should be fun, and for him a major source of fun was challenging authority and testing boundaries, especially those involving driving. A student at UCLA at the time, Lloyd owned a very stylish Plymouth convertible in which he zipped around West Los Angeles, often with an attractive coed in the passenger seat, and sometimes with me riding happily in the rear. I cannot begin to count the number of tickets Lloyd received for things like running red lights, speeding, or other offenses. I remember that he would simply stuff the citation into the already bulging glove compartment and forget about it. I assume that in those pre-computer days, it took a long time for the traffic authorities to catch up to scofflaws. In Lloyd's case, they never did.

While at UCLA, Lloyd lived at his fraternity, Theta Delta Chi, but during school breaks and holidays he would stay with us on Orange Grove, sleeping on a cot in my bedroom. Those were my favorite times, because Lloyd was the only one in our family who seemed to understand that a young boy needed to have fun, and he was a never-ending source of new adventures. If I was still awake when Lloyd came into our shared bedroom and settled under the blankets on his cot, he would tell me stories about his own youth. His stories always seemed to have an element of excitement and thrill that my own life lacked, so I loved to hear of his early adventures. When he was very small, his family still lived in Prescott, Arizona, where his uncle was town sheriff, and where the cowboys would come into town every Saturday night to raise hell. Lloyd told me that his father and mother made him hide under his bed on Saturday nights so he wouldn't be hit by a stray bullet, and he would fall asleep to the sound of random gunfire as the cowboys emptied their pistols into the air. I had never heard a gunshot or known a real sheriff, so I envied my uncle's exciting past. I had only seen cowboys in movies or in the Hollywood Christmas Parade, but my uncle had actually been among them and heard their yells and shouts. When he told stories of his youth, he always added in a shout or two of his own, just so I could know what his own life had sounded like.

When Lloyd had been about to start elementary school, the mines in northern Arizona began to close, so his mother, father and sister were forced to leave Prescott. They moved to Huntington Beach, an oil-producing town south of Los Angeles, where Lloyd's father could get work with the Union Oil Company. Following high school in Huntington Beach, Lloyd entered UCLA, where he was still a student when I was born. Not long after my birth, my mother and father divorced, and my mother moved back in with her parents, Gracie and Patrick. I have early memories of our little household, headed by the powerful Gracie, and consisting of my grandfather, my mother, Lloyd (when he was home from college) and me. This was at the height of the Great Depression, and like so many American families, the Osbornes struggled financially on a daily basis. I know that the only way Lloyd was able to afford attending UCLA was by enrolling in the ROTC program, whereby his college expenses would be paid in exchange for his agreeing to serve in the Army for a set number of years following graduation. Even at my very young age, I remember being confused by the apparent contradiction in Lloyd's life, between his disdain—indeed, hostility—toward the police, and his willingness to serve in such a highly authoritarian institution as the Army. But Lloyd found a way to resolve this conflict.

Lloyd once told me that he did not intend to stay in the Army any longer than necessary—indeed, he had already been offered a civilian job by a fraternity brother, which he intended to accept. However, as long as he was in the Army, he was going to make the best of it, and what he wanted most was to command troops and turn his unit into the best fighting machine possible. His strong rebelliousness took the form of wanting to show senior officers how the Army should really operate, and from the beginning of his military career he excelled. After basic training, he took advanced training as an infantry officer, and was soon assigned to command a unit in the Philippines, then a "protectorate" of the United States.

Although Lloyd was not a regular resident of my Orange Grove complex at the time of this present memoir, he was nonetheless constantly present in everyone's mind, a sort of spectral being. During his times with us while he was still at UCLA, Lloyd injected much-needed youthfulness, energy and humor into everyone's lives. He personified the importance of fun. When he was around, the individual demons of each family seemed to evaporate temporarily. Rosita loved Lloyd, and would prepare special meals full of fresh Southern California fruits for him. Homer, who was the only member of the extended family who had actually served in the military, had an opportunity to tell stories about his own times in the Army. My grandmother and grandfather could bask in the warmth of their only son's obvious success and achievement; Lloyd would be the first in our family to graduate from college.

Very soon, circumstances would drastically change how I thought of Lloyd. Initially, my image of him was based just on my own interactions—"older brother," confidant, pal—but when Lloyd's dangerous situation in the Philippines suddenly dominated all of our thoughts and prayers, a strange thing happened. During the evenings, when my entire family would congregate to listen to the nightly news on the radio, each of the adults would share their own recollections of Lloyd. I had never heard these stories before. As I listened to each person recount their experiences with Lloyd, and how important he was to their lives, my impression of him was changed from "my favorite playmate" to that of a complex, ambitious, hard-charging and energetic personality. Very soon, for each of us, our remembrances of Lloyd would become a source of constant worry, and a window into our deepest emotions.

CHAPTER IX

Infamy

The radio in my apartment was on every evening, but never during the daytime, so the sound of our radio playing loudly early on a Sunday morning was startling. I awoke suddenly and came downstairs to see what was happening; and there, sitting on the floor, were most of my family members. Commie had heard that there was some kind of military crisis and had come over to our apartment with Mary Margaret. Rosita and Homer were both present, as were Charles, Ted and Aunt Fan (who rarely left the sanctuary of her bedroom), and my grandmother and grandfather. My grandmother was trying to hold back tears, but without success. I had never seen her cry before, and it made me feel cold and worried. As soon as I had entered our living room, Rosita had held her finger up to her lips, cautioning me to remain silent. Although I could not initially grasp the details coming out of the radio, I immediately sensed that this was a matter of the most grave seriousness, and I soon understood that our country was under attack. My grandmother's main concern was any news of what was happening on the other side of the Pacific, in the Philippines where her only son was stationed.

For hours, the only news we heard was about the Japanese attack on the U.S. fleet at Pearl Harbor, and on other parts of Hawaii.

Many people in California had recently visited Hawaii, since the Matson ship line had inaugurated frequent and reasonably priced cruises from Los Angeles and San Francisco. Occasionally, one of the news readers would mention that "other attacks" were apparently taking place, but without any specific information. In fact, Japan had carefully planned and was now executing eight major attacks around the Pacific Rim, including the Philippines, which was the primary U.S. Army base in the Pacific, and the British colony of Malaya and the Dutch East Indies (now Indonesia). A large Japanese attack fleet had secretly moved into Philippine waters at the same time aircraft carriers had moved to within a few hundred miles of Hawaii; and within a few hours of the attack on Hawaii, Japanese troops invaded the northern Philippines. Less than two weeks later, 43,000 elite Japanese Army soldiers attacked the main island of Luzon, where Captain William Lloyd Osborne commanded a company of American and Filipino troops.

For hours no one said anything. We stared hypnotically at the big radio while we listened intently to the live broadcast, most of which involved local reporters reading reports received from the AP and UPI news wires, but with an occasional live report from Hawaii. We could tell it was live because there was so much static that we could hardly make out what was being said. When there was no new news to report, the radio reporters would conduct interviews with local politicians and "experts," but as we now know, speculation by so-called experts, who in fact knew nothing but were still anxious to predict what would happen next, would lead to unnecessary hysteria and fear, and even to some very tragic deaths.

Since it was a Sunday morning, the major radio stations, including clear-channel KFI, had only skeleton staffs in the studios when the news first broke. In those days church attendance in L.A. was very high, and many people were already in church or on their way when the news broke. As word of the crisis quickly spread, many churches emptied out as people returned home to be with loved ones and to listen to the latest news on the radio. As the morning wore on, the regular KFI newsmen started to arrive at the station, and we heard more familiar voices telling us the latest news from Hawaii and Washington, D.C. From the start, the news was terrible, and it continued to get worse throughout the day. First we heard that the battleship U.S.S. *California* had been badly damaged, and then we heard that the U.S.S. *Arizona* had exploded. Eyewitness accounts from Honolulu started to come in. Not only had virtually the entire U.S. Pacific naval fleet been destroyed or badly damaged, the Army Air Force base at Hickam Field had also been attacked and many planes destroyed. No one could yet estimate the number of American sailors and soldiers killed, but the newsreaders speculated that it must be in the thousands.

I remember that each of us had a different reaction to the terrible news. For long periods no one would speak, instead listening silently to the increasingly grim reports coming from our radio. Gracie was no longer trying to be brave, and was sobbing continuously. My grandfather was trying to console her; but when he would put his arm around her shoulders, it just made her cry harder. My grandfather's eyes were bloodshot, and his face looked swollen. Aunt Fan, who was sitting in a large armchair, was completely still, with her gaze centered on some unknown and faraway object. Occasionally she would mouth words, but no sound would emanate from her throat. Commie, who normally would have been talking constantly, was totally silent. Interestingly, the only person who seemed not to be in shock was Mary Margaret. She was the one who began to care for the rest of us, as though we were inmates in a kind of mental prison and she was our nurse. Not long after I arrived in our living room, she came over and whispered in my ear, "I want you to go up to your room and put on some clothes" (I was still in my pajamas). "Be sure to pick out long pants and one of your nicer shirts, maybe the blue one with the gold star on the pocket." I did as I was told. When I got back to the living room, there was a bowl of oatmeal waiting for me, on the floor near where I had been sitting. Every few minutes Mary Margaret would disappear into the kitchen and return with a pot of tea and some cups, or a plate of cheese and crackers. Mary Margaret had somehow assumed a role she had never played before: the caretaker for all of us, knowing that despite the deeply disturbing news we were getting from the radio, we still needed refreshment and nourishment.

The foremost concern on everyone's mind was what might happen to Lloyd. We all knew that Lloyd's specific unit was under the command of General Jonathan Wainwright, because when Lloyd had been home on leave he would speak glowingly of the general's intelligence and leadership. What he liked best about General Wainwright was his positive attitude toward the infantry. Lloyd was a firm believer that the infantry was by far the most important part of the entire military, especially when compared to what he called "the flyboys" (in those days what later became the U.S. Air Force was part of the Army), and the "guys riding around on horses" (the U.S. Cavalry, which was in its last year of riding actual horses into battlefields, specifically in the Philippines). But Lloyd's distaste for the flyboys and the guys on horses didn't hold a candle to his total contempt for the Navy ("most of the time they're just cruisin' around somewhere getting lost—and every sailor I've ever known has been dumb as a mule"). Lloyd thought that war was about fighting at close range in hand-to-hand combat, or at least being close enough to the enemy to shoot him.

As Sunday morning turned to afternoon, it became obvious that the Japanese attack had been extremely successful. The United States Pacific fleet had been destroyed or badly damaged, and would be unable to respond to further Japanese aggression. Now, additional concerns were being raised, both on the radio and in the newspaper special editions that were being delivered every few hours. For those of us in Los Angeles, the biggest question was, "Are we next?" A large contributing factor to what would quickly become hysteria was everyone's total ignorance of the power of the Japanese military, especially its navy. No one, at least in my family, had ever talked about the Imperial Japanese Navy as some kind of invincible force, able to mobilize hundreds of fighting ships and simultaneously attack American, British, French and Dutch forces throughout the huge expanses of the Pacific Ocean. Almost overnight, our cherry blossom-tinged impression of Japan changed from complacency—that these seemingly meek Asian people could never threaten the might of the United States and Great Britain—to a combination of awe and fear, that somehow these people had completely surpassed us in naval and air power without us even noticing. (In later years, historians would demonstrate that these same naïve and racist ideas also permeated the U.S. military, which did not take seriously the possibility of Japanese superiority in weaponry. This was especially true of the U.S. Army's air forces in the Philippines.) The only member of our family who seemed to have any idea of what might happen next was Commie, who some months before had volunteered to take a civil defense class. A few days after the attack on Pearl Harbor, Commie would be appointed as the Civil Defense Block Captain for our little part of Orange Grove Avenue.

As night fell that terrible Sunday, my grandmother finally turned off the radio. She said to us, "We must all hold together and support each other. We don't know what is coming and we don't know what has happened to Lloyd, but we all have our responsibilities here. Tomorrow is the start of a new week, and most of us need to continue to do our jobs." At this point, she looked at me. "In particular, we need to take special care to make sure Gary is in a safe place, and fed, and never alone." After everyone had nodded in acceptance, each family went off to deal with their own lives and futures. It was already past my own bedtime, and I was very tired; but when my grandmother had tucked me in and turned off the lights, I remember not being able to sleep for what seemed like a long time. It occurred to me that no day could ever be as terrible as this one had been. But I was wrong.

CHAPTER X

The War Comes to Orange Grove

In the evenings following December 7, we would gather in my grandmother's apartment to listen to the day's news, and discuss the awful things that were happening in Asia and Europe. Of course, our number-one concern was the status of Lloyd and the American troops in the Philippines, but there was seldom any news from there. However, there were constant reports about major Japanese military successes in other parts of Asia. Similarly, the news from Europe was consistently grim, with victory upon victory by the Nazis. Like everyone else in the country, we had been momentarily inspired by President Roosevelt's dramatic "a date which will live in infamy" speech, in which he had asked Congress for a declaration of war, but now it seemed that there was never any good news from anywhere. In the first days of January came the news that the Philippines capital, Manila, near where Lloyd was stationed, had fallen to Japanese troops, while fighting continued in other parts of that beleaguered country.

My daily routine returned to an earlier time, before I had become Commie's sales assistant. During January and February, Commie was gone most days, in training as a civil defense worker. Mary

Margaret, Homer and my grandmother had returned to their jobs, and Ted was somewhere working on a film. When Charles was sober I would spend time with him, but for the most part I was again on my own, riding my bicycle around and observing people's comings and goings. The highlight of most days was breakfast and lunch at Rosita's. At one point I even thought I was learning Spanish, as I was starting to understand part of her constant chatter. I had always looked forward to the visits of Mr. Seiter, but he did not visit during the first weeks of the new year. In retrospect this was a very strange time, because the country was gearing up for what would be the most terrible and costly war in our history, yet most of my family was going about their business as they had for years before. However, this would all change in late February. The war was about to come to our home on Orange Grove Avenue.

* * *

The hysteria started when some Japanese submarines appeared just off the California coastline. Within a few days, some U.S. merchant ships were torpedoed and sunk. We had learned that the destruction of the U.S. Navy fleet at Pearl Harbor had been preceded by Japanese submarines secretly gathering just off the coast of Oahu. Now it appeared that the same thing was happening to us. No one, including the U.S. Navy, knew where the huge Japanese fleet had gone after December 7 or what its next target might be. There was constant word on the radio and in the newspapers that Los Angeles could be the next Pearl Harbor, especially since the ports of Los Angeles and Long Beach were becoming major transportation hubs for moving war material and men to the war in Asia. Each evening at our nightly gatherings, Commie would share with us what he had been told during his training sessions. The information was mostly ominous.

The day after Washington's birthday, on February 23, a Japanese submarine surfaced off the coast of Santa Barbara, just north of Los Angeles. It started shelling an oil field just outside Santa Barbara proper, then disappeared again. As far as we knew, that submarine and many more could now be submerged near the Santa Monica Pier, only a few short miles from our home, ready to shell us. Everyone in my extended family was very tense and worried.

The next night, in the wee hours of February 25, all the newly installed air raid sirens in my city went off. It was incredibly loud and very frightening, and the noise came from all directions. There was a big siren at the corner of Pico and Orange Grove right near our complex, and when it went off it seemed like our whole building would shake to the ground. I had been asleep in bed, but I got up to look out my window and saw Commie coming out of the door of his apartment. He headed off down the block, already dressed in his full Civil Defense regalia. The sounding of the sirens signaled a total blackout for the city, meaning that all lights were supposed to be turned off, curtains drawn tight, and any openings under doors filled with towels, so that even the faint light of a single candle would not escape. Streetlights and traffic signals were all turned off. Cars were supposed to return home immediately, so there would be no headlights that Japanese bombers could use to target our city.

A few minutes after the sirens went off, my neighborhood was changed from a brightly lit friendly place to a dark, mysterious, ominous and very silent wilderness. Not only was it dark, but it seemed that no one was talking or playing radios or walking outside. From my bedroom window I could normally see the bright neon lights of businesses along Pico, and up and down Fairfax, just one block to the west, but now there was nothing but darkness and silence. After a while I climbed into bed and fell into a fitful sleep. I didn't know it, but death and destruction were to be visited on my city that very night.

The fury of war struck Orange Grove Avenue at around three o'clock in the morning. I was suddenly awakened by the deafening roar of huge guns. The sky was brilliant with shells going off. When three or four shells would explode at the same time, the entire sky would light up, almost like full daylight. I had never even known there were big guns in my neighborhood, but somehow the Army, anticipating a possible bombing raid, had placed large anti-aircraft guns all over the city—some in vacant lots, some on trucks, most of them hidden under multicolored cloth. Now it seemed certain that the Japanese were attacking us, and we were trying to shoot down the incoming bombers.

I ran down the stairs to our living room, just as Mary Margaret and Rosita arrived. My grandfather had turned on the radio, which was reporting that spotters had detected incoming planes and several had been shot down. After a few minutes the radio announcer announced, "We've just received a report from the police department that an enemy plane has crashed onto Fairfax Boulevard, in Hollywood." Fairfax was just a block from Orange Grove. I hadn't heard any crash, but with all the constant noise from the guns, it was impossible to tell. Soon the radio reporter told us that casualties had been reported from downtown, Hollywood, and Santa Monica, all near to us. I saw that Mary Margaret and Rosita were both crying. Rosita said that Homer had gone out to find Commie and to help him with his duties. After a while, Charles came in. He didn't look at all well; apparently he was in the early stage of a periodic recovery.

In later years, cynics and critics had a great deal of fun satirizing what was sardonically known as "The Battle of Los Angeles." It turned out there had never been any Japanese airplanes over Los

Angeles that night, nor would there ever be. The whole episode was triggered by an erroneous sighting of "something" in the sky by a soldier who happened to have his finger on an aircraft gun activator. Everything that followed was a case of hysteria. However, there was nothing whatsoever funny about being in the center of a darkened Los Angeles at 3:00 a.m. on February 25, 1942, believing that bombs were falling, with cannon fire booming, huge spotlights searching the sky for enemy planes, and terror everywhere. In fact, an incredible number of explosive shells—more than 1,400 of them—were fired into the sky over Los Angeles that night, and most of them exploded. Some that did not explode over the city came back to earth on buildings and houses, which were set afire. Several people were killed or literally died of fright in the ensuing chaos. No one in my little family had ever seen or heard explosions of this magnitude before. For me, and perhaps for thousands of other children in Los Angeles, the terror of that night was never to be forgotten. In later years I learned a very important lesson; namely, that "history" as written by academics who were not present does not necessarily reflect the real-life experiences of those who lived through a particular event or time. I have never seen any history of the 1940s that comes close to describing the almost unendurable terror that I and many other children experienced that horrible February night. My own reaction to the terror of that night, as I cowered in my grandmother's arms, was to experience a taste in my mouth that I had never known before. I have since thought of it as the bitter taste of deep and abiding fear. I have only experienced it a very few times since that night—once when coming face-to-face with an angry rattlesnake while climbing a desert sand dune, and another time when I was sure the plane on which I was flying was going to crash. Now, when I see one of the movies that make fun of L.A.'s "hysteria" on that February night, I have another reaction—anger and rage. I feel like grabbing the filmmaker by the throat and yelling in their face, "How can you laugh at something that made little children quiver in terror??"

CHAPTER XI

The Meeting

As dawn arrived, the adults were still listening to the radio, but I had fallen asleep on Rosita's lap. When I awoke, the radio was reporting that the Japanese attack appeared to be over. The newsreader said that six Japanese planes had been shot down. The reporter also told us that fires were raging all over the city, and that hospitals were reporting that the victims of the previous night's bombing were being treated and that there had been some deaths.

Early in the afternoon, I was outside on my bike, when the long black limousine I knew belonged to Mr. Seiter pulled up in front of our complex. He and another man emerged from the back seat, and Mr. Seiter said to me, "Hello, Gary. I hope you weren't too scared by last night's events. I have to meet with your family on some important matters, which aren't for children to hear, but will you do something for me? Will you tell everyone in your family that I'd like to meet with them in my brother's apartment right away?" With that, he headed down the path to Charles and Ted's apartment, while I ran to my own apartment, and then to Rosita's and then Commie's apartments.

I wonder if most children try to listen in on conversations that are not intended for them? Especially if it involves their parents or might be something about themselves? In my own case, when doing my bicycle rounds in the courtyard, I had found that my families often kept their windows open due to the nice weather, and it was easy to overhear conversations if I lingered near the windows outside. Perhaps I was an especially nosy child? My grandparents never argued or exchanged unpleasant words in public, but I had learned that when they assumed they were completely alone, they engaged in some fairly vigorous disagreements, which I found intriguing to listen in on. I had also overheard Charles and Ted's frequent arguments, and Commie and Mary Margaret's more subdued confrontations. I was now very curious to hear what important news Mr. Seiter had to share; but since I had been prohibited from attending, I crept to a spot just outside the Apartment 3 living room window, which was conveniently shielded by tall plants.

The first to speak was Mr. Seiter. He had a very powerful and persuasive way of speaking, which he had told me he used to "shape up" the actors in the many films he had directed. He now said, "I have to tell you that our situation is very serious and perilous. The events of last night were only the beginning. This war will be very long and very painful. I already know that this morning's reports of a major Japanese bombing raid aren't true. But that's not the important thing, because we do know for sure that Japan has the capacity and the will to mount a major attack on our west coast, and that we simply aren't ready to defend ourselves. But there's something even more ominous than that. The Germans are planning to invade England. If they succeed, soon after that they may attack and occupy New York."

Here Mr. Seiter paused. When he began speaking again, his tone sounded even more dramatic. "As I told you when we were all together on Thanksgiving, my brother Charles and I are Jews, and many of the people I work with in making movies are as well. If the Nazis succeed in attacking New York, and if the Japanese do the same here, our lives won't be worth anything. I've spent all day speaking with many friends, some of whom are truly terrified. The last stop I made before coming here was at Arnold's house—I mean Professor Schoenberg. He's an Austrian Jew, and he knows that many of his family and friends back home are already dead, or wishing they were. Arnold himself was almost hysterical. Earlier today I met with some of my Jewish friends from Poland and Germany, who moved to L.A. because they thought this would be the safest place in the world. But last night they felt that the security of their lives here had been shattered."

At this point Mr. Seiter paused again. When he resumed, he was speaking in a softer, conspiratorial tone. I had to strain my ears to hear what he said. "Unfortunately, it's very possible that America may become unsafe for Jews. If the Nazis install some rabid anti-Semite like Henry Ford or Charles Lindbergh as president, our lives will be over. I must tell you, as a secret just among us, that I'm part of a group of producers and directors and a few studio heads who are making urgent plans to move our families to a safer location. We need to make plans now. The Jews of Europe didn't believe what was about to happen to them, and now thousands of them have been murdered in cold blood. We here must prepare for the worst, and we must do it now. I can't say anything more right now, except that some of my friends and I have purchased land where we can find more safety than here, and if the worst happens we must be prepared to leave at a moment's notice. If we have to go, I want my brother to go with me, and also Ted and of course, Fan. As I told you a few weeks ago at Thanksgiving, I know that you all mean the world to Charles. He thinks of you as his family because you have helped him in so many ways. He thinks of Gary as his own son, and Gracie and Pat as his own parents. So, what I've come to say to all of you is, if we need to go, we want all of you to come with us."

There was complete silence in the room. From my hiding spot I could not see into the room, but I thought I heard someone sobbing. Then I heard Mr. Seiter say something to the effect that he would be back in touch soon, signaling that the meeting had come to a close. I quickly vacated my hiding spot and returned to my previous position at the entrance to our complex. Within seconds I heard the door to Apartment 3 open, and Mr. Seiter came striding out with a serious expression on his face. He walked quickly to his limousine, but just as he was about to get in, he suddenly stopped, turned, and looked directly at me. For a moment I was afraid he was going to chastise me for having eavesdropped, but instead he walked over to where I was sitting on my bicycle, knelt down on one knee so he could look me directly in the eye, and said, "Gary, you're a very important part of my brother's life. He thinks of you almost like his own son. Now my brother needs as much help as we can give him, especially from you and me. Can I count on you?"

Of course I nodded 'yes.' At that moment Mr. Seiter took my little hand in his larger one and shook it up and down. It made me feel that Mr. Seiter was treating me as a full adult, which in a sense I think he was. With that, Mr. Seiter stood up, quickly walked back to his car, and was gone in a matter of seconds. I remained sitting on my bicycle, transfixed, for many minutes. The power of William Seiter's voice, manner, strength and empathy had convinced me that I now had a greater responsibility to help Charles.

* * *

Early one morning a few days after the Battle of Los Angeles, I saw Mrs. O'Grady passing our house, coming back from Pico, her shopping cart full of groceries. I had not seen her for several weeks, and she looked very different from the last time I had seen her—somehow older and more frail. She saw me, and signaled for me to come over to the sidewalk. I got off my bicycle and stood facing her, noticing that I was almost as tall as she was. She looked at me for a long time, and then started crying. She started to speak in a halting and choked voice: "I should tell you that each day I look forward to seeing you and having a chance to say hello. I almost feel like we have become real friends. Now I see that you have grown so much and are almost a young man." She reached into her purse, pulled out a tissue and dabbed at her eyes. "But this may be the last time I see you. I cannot live here anymore, with this constant fear. You see, I have lived this before, back in my old country."

Her voice shaking, she continued, "When I was a young girl, soldiers suddenly arrived in my village and went house to house, shooting people. My mother pushed me into the back of a kitchen cabinet and told me not to move for any reason. I did as I was told, and I could hear gunshots when the soldiers got to our house. They never looked in the place where I was hiding, and after many hours, I came out. My mother and father and three brothers had been killed and my older sister was nowhere to be seen. All I could think of was to get away from that house of death. I took as much food as I could carry in a bag, and hid in the forest for many days. Sometime later I was found by some other survivors from my village and all of us hid in that forest for a long time, until we were able to escape to the sea, and then to Sweden."

Mrs. O'Grady had stopped crying, but there was great sorrow in her voice as she said, "I thought that Los Angeles would be a safe place, but now it is not. Two nights ago I realized that we could be invaded at any time. I cannot hide in a kitchen cabinet a second time. My husband and I are leaving today for Nebraska. My husband has a brother there who told us we could stay with him on his farm. If the Japs and the Nazis invade, that will be the last place they get to, and by then there will not be anywhere safe for us anyway. My husband and I have a pact. We will never be captured. We will die in each other's arms first."

For a long time Mrs. O'Grady said nothing. Then she walked over and gave me a very strong hug, and was gone down the street, pulling her grocery cart. I walked over to the stairs leading up into Rosita's apartment and sat down on one of the steps, staring into space. I felt like crying, but could not. I have never forgotten that moment, or my last sight of Mrs. O'Grady hurrying away down Orange Grove.

CHAPTER XII

"The Worst Day Forever"

The days after the Battle of Los Angeles were filled with tension and anxiety for everyone. Mr. Seiter's talk with my family had brought home the true danger of the war and what it meant to our daily lives. The dark reality of the world had penetrated the fantasy of the Southern California lifestyle. After all, life consisted of things beyond sunshine and going to the beach, and for the first time we truly understood that death and destruction could happen to us. Indeed, some of our fellow Los Angeles residents had already died, and others were still in the hospital, fighting for their lives.

Not long after Mr. Seiter's visit, as I was riding my bicycle around our complex, a brown military car pulled up, and two Army officers in full dress got out of the back seat. One of them asked me if I knew where Patrick Henry Osborne lived, and I motioned to my own apartment. One of the officers knocked on the door, and Gracie answered and ushered the officers into our living room. I tried to follow the officers into the room, but one of them told my grandfather that I should not be present. My grandmother told me to go to my bedroom until she came for me. As I started for my room, I quickly looked into our living room, and I noticed that my grandfather had turned very white.

I went to my room as told and waited for what seemed a long time. Finally, I heard our front door open. From my bedroom window I could see the two Army officers walking slowly toward their car. While they were still standing on the sidewalk, I saw Commie come quickly out of his apartment and run toward them. He spoke to the officers for a few moments before they got in their car and were driven away. I could hear what sounded like moans coming from my living room, and I also heard sobbing. After a few minutes, I heard our front door open again, and my grandmother walked across our courtyard to Commie and Mary Margaret's apartment, and soon returned. A short time later, Commie and Mary Margaret had collected Rosita and Homer, and Charles and Aunt Fan, and they were all heading to my apartment.

After a few minutes, Commie knocked at my bedroom door, which occurred to me as very unusual, since usually no one ever knocked before coming into my room. I opened the door, and Commie said in a very somber voice, "Today you need to be a man. Today you need to be with all of us, not as a child, but as much of an adult as you can be. And you must be very very strong. Can you do that?"

My heart was beating so fast and hard that I was sure Commie could hear it, but I told him, "I will be strong, I promise you."

Commie led me into our living room, where everyone was already seated. He then spoke with a directness and eloquence I had never heard before. He said, "You may have seen the two Army officers that came to give Gracie and Pat the news of Lloyd. I'm sorry to say that he's now classified as 'missing and presumed dead.' Lloyd's name was not among those released by the Army as having been captured, and there's no indication that he's among the living prisoners. We know that thousands of American soldiers have been killed in the invasion and fall of Bataan, and the Red Cross has been given the names of those who are in prisoner of war camps. The officers told me that since Lloyd was an infantry captain, he would have been leading his company into battle, and might well have been one of the first killed. So we all have to acknowledge that our beloved Lloyd is most likely dead, and that, given all the chaos and confusion in the Philippines, his body may never be found."

Here Commie paused and looked at each one of us individually. To Mary Margaret he said, "You must give Gracie all the love and support that you have within you, for she has suffered a great shock and a great loss." My grandmother was still sobbing, now quietly but very steadily. Mary Margaret came over to her and put her arms around her, and held her tightly for a long time. To Homer, Commie said, "You and I and Charles must work together to help Pat in this hour of his greatest need. He has lost his only son, and in a way, Lloyd was a son to us all." Homer and Charles both rose, went over to my grandfather, and sat down beside him on the couch. My grandfather was still very white, and looked to me to be in shock; but when Charles took his hand, my grandfather said, quietly but very clearly, "This is the worst day, forever." I can never forget those words.

Commie then walked over to where I was sitting on the floor, and he asked me to stand up. He spoke to me as he had never done before, almost as equal to equal: "You and I have had many adventures together, and you have helped me on many of my house sales. I know that you are mature beyond your years, and that you can be very serious. Normally, this would be a time for you to be a child and to do childish things, but this is not a normal time; and our family"—he gestured around the room—"needs you to be as much of an adult as you can be. I know that you can do it and that you will do it." My emotions at this point did not allow me to even form words or to speak, but I could stand as straight and tall as possible, which is what I did.

CHAPTER XIII

Gracie Goes to War

Early the next morning, my grandmother came into my room and awakened me. She looked very tired, as though she had not slept at all. She said to me, "Please get dressed right now and come down to the living room." I did as I was told, and when I got downstairs, everyone in the family was there, even Aunt Fan and Charles, who I noticed was shaking slightly.

We all sat without speaking for many minutes. Finally, my grandmother stood up and everyone watched intently to see what she was going to do. She started speaking in a very low voice that I had not heard before. This is what she said: "Lloyd always wanted to be a soldier, from when he was just about Gary's age. He didn't want to fly and he didn't want to be at sea. He wanted to be in the Army, on the ground. He wanted to lead men in combat. That's exactly what he trained himself for. And now, Lloyd has been deprived of his destiny. He's been denied the opportunity to fulfill his dream. He was my only son. I believe it to be my duty to take his place. I've decided. Tomorrow I'm going to join the Army. If I succeed, I'll try to be as near the front as I can be. I will try to do honor to my son's memory."

I can never forget that moment, to the end of my life. Every person in the room was transfixed, speechless, amazed, virtually open-mouthed. No one spoke for a very long time. Finally my grandmother said, "I read in the paper that there are many Army jobs that men are doing now, but if women could do those jobs, like driving trucks or repairing things or cooking or being part of medical units, or even flying, then the men could go into combat, where they're urgently needed. I read that Congress has just passed an act to create a women's unit for the Army, so that many more men can be moved to combat. I want to be among the first to volunteer. I'll do anything they ask so that more men can go up into a fighting unit."

At this point Mary Margaret put her arms around my grandmother and said, "Gracie, what you want to do is wonderful, and very brave. My only worry is that I think there must be an upper age limit on joining the Army, so I hope you won't get your hopes up too much. There are lots of other things all of us can do to help the war effort."

My grandmother replied, "I know about the age limit, but I have a plan." And with that mysterious statement, our meeting was concluded. None of us really believed that my grandmother could actually do what she hoped to do.

Early the next morning my grandmother told my grandfather and me, "I may be gone all day, but there's food in the icebox, and I've asked Rosita to come over and make sure you eat properly. Don't worry about me." By late afternoon my grandmother still had not returned, and we were all getting worried, but Commie told us that he was sure she would be back before too long. It was well after dark when she finally returned home. Everyone in our family immediately came over to our apartment, except for Ted, who was still away. When we all had gathered in our living room, my grandmother stood before us and said, "Early this morning I volunteered for the Army. The recruiter tried to turn me away because I was a woman, but I told him that Congress had passed a new law and somehow he believed me. But then he asked my age. I told him that my birth certificate had been destroyed in a fire, which is true, because the courthouse in Prescott burned down many years ago. I guess some of the men also don't have proof of age, because the recruiter gave me a form to sign that asked what my true age was. Of course I lied. But they didn't ask any more questions.

"They told me and one or two other women to wait in an anteroom. We waited there for many hours. Finally, a soldier came in and said that they had found a woman doctor to give us physicals. A few minutes later an older woman came into the room and told us she had just been called, but had no instructions on how to administer a physical, so she would just make sure we didn't have any obvious diseases. I think the doctor realized I wasn't exactly in my twenties or thirties, but she didn't say anything. The exam took about ten minutes. Then we waited some more, and finally the same soldier came back and told us we had all passed our physicals, and that we should join the men in another room. Then an amazing thing happened. A senior officer came into the room and said to us, 'Thank you all for volunteering to serve your country. As you know, we are now in great danger, and we need men right now. Normally it takes a long time to be accepted into the Army, but this is not a usual time. For any of you who are sure you want to join the United States Army, I am now prepared to swear you in. So, let's do this. Please raise your right hands.'

"All the men, and the few of us women, raised our hands and said 'we do' when prompted. The officer then said, 'Congratulations, men, you are now members of the greatest fighting unit on the face of the earth.' He seemed to have forgotten that a few of us were women, but that didn't matter, and we women hugged each other. As of tonight, I am Buck Private Grace Elaine Osborne, United States Women's Army Auxiliary Corps. I'm now a WAAC. I report to Union Station next Tuesday to catch a train to a base in Iowa, to start basic training. That is where Lloyd went for part of his infantry training, after he finished basic training at Fort Benning. Tomorrow I'll quit my job at the May Company. I'm counting on all of you to take good care of Gary."

For the second time in two days, our entire family was speechless. We all just stared at my grandmother. No one had really believed she could or would join the Army, not only because everyone (except me) knew that she was way too old, but mostly because we couldn't visualize her in an Army uniform, marching around with her unit, saluting senior officers, going on all-day and all-night hikes. But everyone had underestimated her. I think everyone saw her now in a completely different light. She had said she would take Lloyd's place, and now she would. Homer said that of course she would have to make it through basic training, which could be very tough, but somehow we knew she would. Later, Homer told me privately that he was sure Gracie would try to be in the most dangerous place she could. He said he had read that some WAACs might be assigned to front-line combat units as field nurses, which I later found out was true. Later in the war, there were many WAACs killed or wounded while working in mobile field hospitals, especially those working as surgical assistants.

Commie decided that our entire family should give Gracie a great sendoff. There were going-away parties for the next several days, most of which I was not invited to because there was a lot of drinking. Before dawn on Tuesday morning, all of us except Aunt Fan, Ted and Charles, who had fallen off the wagon during a weekend party and had disappeared, piled into cars and made a little pilgrimage to Union Station. When we arrived in the cavernous central lobby, there were what looked like several hundred women with suitcases, most with families there to see them off. Even I noticed that virtually all of the women looked very young, like teenagers or high school girls. Many were wearing bobby socks, a craze at that time.

After a few minutes, a soldier in uniform announced through a megaphone, "All WAAC recruits go to track number four. At the back of the train will be a sergeant with a clipboard. Give him your name, then board the train. You'll all be American soldiers pretty soon. Good luck to you all." The gate to track number four was guarded by military police and only recruits were allowed through, so we had to say our goodbyes outside. Mary Margaret and Rosita were both crying, and I think I was too, but Gracie shushed us, saying, "Come on, don't be sissies. I'll be fine, and I'll write as soon as I can." It seemed that all the other recruits were being seen off by mothers and fathers, and even grandparents. I'm pretty sure that Gracie was the only one being seen off by her grandson.

CHAPTER XIV

News from Des Moines

Gracie had promised us that she would write as often as she could, and she was true to her word. Her first letter arrived in the afternoon mail less than a week after she had left Union Station. It was a Sunday, and most of the family was home. Gracie had addressed the envelope to her husband Pat, but the letter inside was addressed to "My Dearest Family." My grandfather gave the letter to Charles to read, and we all listened to Charles' deep voice with rapt attention. Charles read Gracie's words:

> *I think there are several hundred of us here in Des Moines. It is a wonderful group; we all help each other. Many of the girls have never been away from home before. They were very homesick the first couple of nights and some were crying, but the rest of us talked to them and made little jokes. The girls all call me "Mom," which is OK with me. No one knows I'm actually a grandma, which is also OK with me. The very first thing that happened when we got off the train was they took us to this medical place, and we all had to take off our clothes, and a lot of the girls were very embarrassed, but not me. I'm too old to worry about things like that. Some women nurses checked us for lice and diseases, and then a doctor gave everyone six or seven shots.*

> Ouch! Then they gave us our "uniforms," which are just fatigues. You might wonder how I have time to write. Well, the commanding officer told us we should write letters home several times a week, and that time would be set aside for this purpose. Since we are the first women in the U.S. Army and many people don't think women should serve in the Army, he said it was important we tell all the people back home that we are being treated well. Well, our time is almost up, so I'll have to close. But I guess you'll be getting quite a few letters from me. Love to you all. Gracie.

Every evening during the next ten weeks, when everyone was home from work, we would automatically gather in my apartment to see if a letter had arrived from Gracie. If one had come that day, my grandfather would give it to either Charles or Commie to read. These readings became the absolute highlights of everyone's day. Often someone would ask Charles or Commie to read the entire missive through again. Gracie was able to report, simply and dramatically, on all the activities of her basic training, which was modeled on what male soldiers went through at Fort Benning, and was run by male officers who believed that if these "girls" were going to be actual soldiers, they had to pass the same physical trials as the men. From the beginning, we noticed that the Army was putting great emphasis on physical training. In fact, one of the most important Army manuals for fitness was written during this time, and was based on those early days of preparing women—who were supposedly weak and much less fit than men—for possibly strenuous jobs so that men could be released for combat.

In one of her letters, Gracie told us, "One thing is very funny. Most of the sergeants who are training us try to be very tough and mean, and like to yell in our faces when we are lined up. I think most of them used to train men down at Fort Benning and are using the same tactics on us. But some of the girls start to cry if the sergeant yells in their face, and it obviously makes the sergeant feel bad, and he usually says something like, 'Don't worry, honey, you'll be OK.' The rest of us try not to smile, but we are laughing inside. The other thing is that many of the girls are really young and pretty, and the sergeant likes to flirt with them a little bit, so he can't pretend to be too mean. So, I think we're getting off easier than the guys down at Fort Benning."

Another time Gracie wrote:

> *Last night was our first all-night 20-mile hike. Just as we were preparing for bed, five sergeants came into our barracks and said, 'If you girls are in the field at some base and ordered to move forward or retreat immediately, you will have to grab your things and hike all night, and that is what we're going to do tonight.' We all got dressed and filled our backpacks with water and medicines, and then they had us hike through the whole night in the dark. A lot of the girls had a really hard time, and some girls' feet were bleeding, and we all had scratches from going through undergrowth. The stronger of us helped the others, and we all made it. And I mean every single one of us made it. After the march we hadn't had any sleep at all, but just after dawn we had to assemble. As we stood at attention, a jeep pulled up, and our commanding officer got out. He said to us: 'I am going to tell you the truth. When General Miller asked me to accept this assignment of training women for the United States Army, I pleaded with him not to make me do it. But he wouldn't release me, so I had to take a job that I didn't want. But now, after more than five weeks of training, I wouldn't want any other job in the United States Army. You women have proven that you are real soldiers. When I trained men at Fort Benning, after a 20-mile hike, we always had to go out and pick up some guys who had*

quit, or just couldn't do it or were sick. In all my years, I have never seen a unit where every single individual successfully made it back to base after 20 miles. You women are strong. Truly strong. And you are going to make great American soldiers. Congratulations.' As you can imagine, a lot of us were almost in tears, we were so proud. Well, our writing time is up for today. More soon. Love to all. Gracie.

For those of us sitting around in my apartment that night, there was certainly not a dry eye—though these were tears of happiness and pride.

Near the end of Gracie's ten-week basic training, we received our last letter. This time Mary Margaret read it to us:

Dearest Family. Basic training is almost over. Not one single girl has washed out. A few were on the borderline, but the strongest among us worked with them. Our commanding officer says we are probably the only unit in many years where no one has washed out. Compared to ten weeks ago, we are all very different people. We are strong, we are united, and we are ready for anything. And I mean anything. The men told us at the beginning that they were going to put us through hell, and they expected many of us to fail. They did put us through hell, but we hung together, and we are all much stronger than before. Some of the girls came to Des Moines with baby fat, but no one has baby fat any more. I'm pretty sure I am the oldest girl here, but age doesn't matter for anything anymore. It is what you have inside you that counts. We will all get a short home leave when we finish here, before we go on to other assignments. So I will see you all in a few days. The Army will cable families to let you know when and where we arrive. Love as always, Gracie.

After Mary Margaret finished reading, Rosita asked her to read the letter over again, which she did. Then Commie said, "We all have to be at Union Station when Gracie comes back. We'll have balloons and signs to welcome her home. I'll take care of it." Several days later we again had a pilgrimage to Union Station to await the arrival of Gracie's train. We all remembered what it had been like when the new recruits had assembled more than two months previously, but this day would be even more unforgettable for all of us, and I'm sure for the families of the other girls as well.

As before, Army soldiers prevented us from meeting the train directly, so everyone had to wait outside the gate to Track 4. We could hear the train pulling into the station and the squeal of brakes as it stopped. A few minutes later, the hundreds of us waiting outside the gate witnessed an event of such dramatic power that I doubt anyone could ever forget it as long as they lived. I know I never could. An Army officer stood in front of the closed gate and announced, "Ladies and gentlemen, mothers and fathers, please welcome home one of the very first contingents of the United States Women's Army Corps," at which point the gate was opened, and, in single file, in marched the most impressive group of soldiers imaginable. Each and every one was in full Army uniform, perfectly tailored in dark green matching jacket and trousers and a tie, and each had a medal attached above the pocket over her heart. Each woman wore a cap, at exactly the same angle, and their hair was all in the same style, short and military but somehow still feminine. They marched in formation, in exact step. It was an amazing and heart-rending sight. We could recall that day, just a few months before, when many girls in their late teens or early twenties, some in bobby socks, had gone through that same gate heading toward their train. Now here marched the same girls, really no longer girls but now women, fighting women, women of the United States Army. And there, close to the front of the line, was Gracie. When we saw her, we all jumped up and down and screamed and yelled as loud as we could. As the women came through the gate, they were surrounded by family members, and there were many hugs and kisses and little groups of celebrants talking excitedly. When Gracie came through the gate, we all rushed over to her and tried to hug her at the same time. But then an incredible thing happened. Once the other girls had been greeted by their families, many of them looked around the great Union Station lobby and, once they had spotted Gracie, they came over to her. As each approached, Gracie would greet her by name and give her a hug and shake her hand. I saw that with many of the girls, Grace would whisper something into her ear for only her to hear. In that moment we saw Gracie for who she truly was—a leader and a hero.

It was a joyous and marvelous day. We didn't realize that in the not-too-distant future, Gracie would write letters of sorrowful condolence to the parents of four of the young girls she had helped and befriended during their time in Des Moines, girls for whom she had been "Mom" during the hard physical challenges of basic training. These girls, now women, would give their lives in the service of their country.

CHAPTER XV

To The Front

When the family got home from Union Station, everyone wanted Gracie to tell us everything that had happened since she had left many weeks before; but when we had all gathered in the living room of my apartment, we were surprised when Ted stood up and said, "I think Gracie should have a little time to herself right now. I'm sure she's been through a lot, and that she'll eventually tell us all about it. But for right now, I think we should let her just be with Pat and Gary. Maybe we can all get together tomorrow?" Gracie seemed relieved, and suddenly she looked tired. She said, "Ted's right. It was a long train ride from Des Moines, almost two days, and none of us girls could sleep because there was so much for us to talk about. But I thank you all for coming to see me today. It means so much to me to have all of you as my family. As Ted says, let's get together tomorrow." And with that, Ted, Fan, Charles and everyone else reluctantly gave Gracie a final hug and filed out of our apartment. I saw on our big clock that it was already 9:30 p.m.

The next morning I was awakened by the sounds of excited talking from downstairs. I dressed as quickly as I could and went down to the living room. Commie, Ted and Homer were all looking at a copy of one of Los Angeles' newspapers. There, on the front page, was a big photo of yesterday's arrival of the WAACs at Union

Station. The banner headline said, "FAMILIES GREET RETURN OF AMERICA'S FIRST WOMEN SOLDIERS." And there, in the foreground of the photo, was unmistakably Gracie. The photo must have been taken just as Gracie came through the gate, right before we all descended on her. We hadn't even realized there were reporters and photographers present. We were all excited and thrilled at the publicity, but not Gracie. She said, "This doesn't mean anything, not at all. We haven't proven ourselves to be good soldiers yet, but we will soon. And, when some of us die, as will happen, the ideas of what women can do will change." When Gracie used the word "die," we all stopped celebrating the meaningless newspaper publicity and prepared ourselves for a more somber future.

As the morning wore on, the telephone started to ring with calls from newspaper reporters, wanting to interview Gracie. Apparently some of the other new WAACs had told stories about the "mom" among them who had helped so many, but had also out-hiked and outworked most of her fellow recruits. But Gracie was not interested in publicity. It was only the next day, when a female reporter from a newspaper somewhere back east managed to track down our street and apartment number, that Gracie was willing to give a short interview. I think part of her reluctance to speak with reporters was that she didn't want to admit she was actually a grandmother, nor did she want to have to lie about her real age, which was almost 15 years older than the then upper age limit for joining the WAACs.

Gracie spent almost the entire first day back home telling all of us stories about what it had been like at Fort Des Moines and about her many adventures. But when Mary Margaret asked her to tell us what she had been whispering to the other girls when they had arrived home the day before, she demurred, saying simply, "I guess I had something to tell each girl, and I wanted it to be just between them and me." Charles asked her what the hardest time had been. She thought for a while, and then said, "In about the eighth week, a new sergeant joined our training team, and he told us, 'Down at Fort Benning, we always spend at least one night out in the swamps with the snakes and gators to find out who's a man and who's still a boy.' Of course he was just trying to scare us, but lo and behold, it starting raining the very next day, and he told us that we would have to spend the night outside on a long hike. Of course, we knew they don't have alligators around Des Moines, and not many snakes either, so we weren't that scared, but we didn't love the idea of hiking all night in the rain. But by that time we were toughened up, and we all made it just fine. Everyone, that is, except the new sergeant, who was chilled to the bone and got sick the next day, and had to be taken to the infirmary. Of course, none of us girls laughed in front of our trainers, but just among ourselves we had a great time. One of the girls was a good actress, and she pretended to be the sergeant, acting miserable and shivering. I'm glad none of the men saw us making fun of them. By that time we were pretty sure we were as tough as any of them."

Later that day, after Gracie had told story after story, she said, "I want to tell you what my first assignment will be, but I don't actually know yet. On Tuesday I'll go down to the L.A. headquarters to find out. I recently learned that there's another group of women called the Army Nurse Corps, formed many years ago, and even though they're not officially part of the Army and don't go through basic training, some of them are already being sent to the front. So a lot of the WAAC girls I did basic training with may end up doing clerical work, or working as cooks or drivers, so men in these roles can be reassigned to combat, where they're badly needed. But I want to be at the front. That's where Lloyd was, and where I want to be. I've even thought about asking to be transferred to the Nurse Corps. But I'll find out more in a day or two. The main thing is that I want to get going."

Two days later, Gracie left early in the morning in full uniform to take the bus to one of the U.S. Army bases in Los Angeles. She was gone all day. When she got back early in the evening, all of us in the family were waiting in Rosita and Homer's dining room, where Rosita had prepared a colorful meal of Cuban rice and beans and chicken. When Gracie came in, everyone wanted desperately to hear her news, but Commie had told us we should wait until after dinner, so we all sat down. Commie said grace: "Lord, we thank you for this fellowship, and we thank you for the food that we are about to consume. Lord, we ask for your special protection of our sister and friend Gracie as she starts on a new path, in the service of our country." We all said "Amen," and within seconds Rosita had filled the table with an incredible feast.

When we had all had our fill, Gracie cleared her throat and started to speak. "I think you all may be interested in what happened today. I was expecting to meet with a sergeant. When I got to the base office, there was indeed a sergeant waiting for me, but he told me to follow him, and he took me to a very nice office where a major was sitting at his desk looking through papers. When he looked up at me, I saluted him and he saluted me back, and he told me to sit down. He said his name was Montgomery. He cut right to the chase and asked, 'Private Osborne, are you the mother of Captain William Lloyd Osborne?' I was shocked that he would know that, but of course I said yes. The major then said, 'Private Osborne, I'm so sorry that your son is presumed dead. I did in fact spend time with Captain Osborne when both of us were in basic training. He was the toughest man in our company, and we all respected him. And, Private Osborne, I see by your records from Fort Des Moines that you're just as strong and tough as your son.'

"At this point the major peered at one piece of paper and then another, and then he started to smile. He said, 'I see that your son was born in 1913,' and then, looking at the other piece of paper, he continued, 'And, I see by your own enlistment record that you must have been, let's see, about five years old when your son was born?' His smile got even bigger, and he said, 'I think perhaps we should keep this remarkable fact just between the two of us?' Of course I nodded in agreement. Then he said, 'To be honest with you, Private Osborne, I know that you've requested an assignment close to a combat zone, but I hope you can understand that if you should be killed, it would be very bad for morale. We're already trying to prevent brothers of men killed in combat from being sent into danger, and if a mother and her son were both to be killed, well, the publicity would be very bad. There are other things you can do that will be even more valuable to the war effort. The evaluations from your basic training were very high, and we think you can serve in a very important role. If you're willing, I'll try to work it out in a day or two. Is that acceptable to you, Private Osborne?' I told the major that it was.

"Then he stood up, so I did too. I saluted him and turned to leave the room, but just as I got to the door, the major said something that moved me very deeply. He said, 'Private Osborne, after meeting you, I now know exactly why you've joined the Army. You want to take your son's place. If I should be killed in this war, my own mother would want to do exactly the same thing. Of course, I would tell her not to do it, and I would hope her family wouldn't let her...but like you, I think she would find a way.' At that moment his face looked like that of a little boy. I saluted him again and left the room quickly because I didn't want the major to see that I had tears in my eyes."

When my grandmother had finished speaking, there was total silence in the room. It seemed that all the questions we had been wanting to ask had somehow evaporated in the power and drama of Gracie's story. Once again, we were in silent awe of the new and entirely unexpected life that Gracie was leading. We all understood that the next chapter had not yet been written, but that its time was just about to start.

The next day, around sunset, a telegram arrived for Gracie. She showed it to us. It read: "Private Osborne. It is very important that I meet with you tomorrow. Please come to my office at 4:00 p.m. Thank you. Major Paul Montgomery." My grandmother arose early the next day and spent the morning ironing her Army uniform, polishing her shoes, and fixing her hair. Shortly after lunch, she walked up to Pico to catch the bus to the Army base. Commie had offered to drive her, but she said riding the bus gave her time to think, and besides, she knew Commie had a lot of important things to do with the Civil Defense. As evening approached, the family once again gathered in Rosita and Homer's apartment to await Gracie's return. Finally, just after dark, Gracie came in the door. As with the night before, we enjoyed a delicious meal prepared by Rosita, and then waited for Gracie to speak.

She told us, "I really don't know how to describe what happened today, and actually, there are a few things that I can't tell you, but I'll tell you what I can. There were quite a few people at the meeting today, including Major Montgomery, some other officers, and a woman from the Army Nurse Corps. Apparently there've been some big problems between the Army Nurse Corps—they call it the ANC—and the regular Army over the formation of the WAAC that I'm part of. The senior officers in the Nurse Corps are women, but currently most of the senior officers in the WAAC are men, because we haven't had time to promote women to be officers. Many of the nurses are unhappy, because they think they're the ones putting their lives in danger in combat zones, and they're afraid they'll have to start taking orders from us WAACs, since we're regular Army and they're not. So the Army is setting up a liaison team to try to work things out, and they want me to be part of it, even though I'm still just a private. The colonel said life experience was more important than rank right now. One of the other officers said they want me to do a fact-finding mission, including some details I can't repeat, and that was pretty much that. After the meeting, Major Montgomery took me aside and told me he had already put in for a promotion for me. Then he told me the best thing of all. He said that my fact-finding mission would involve sending me to meet with lots of ANC nurses, and some would be in combat areas. And then he gave me a knowing smile and said, 'Please don't get killed, because it'll be my ass if you do.' I smiled back at him and told him I'd try very hard not to be killed."

We all sat there, stunned. I think our feelings had gone from elation and pride that Gracie would be meeting with senior Army officers and be part of a very important liaison team, to great worry and concern over the possibility that Gracie could be exposed to danger and even death in a combat war zone. Finally Charles said, "Gracie, you're very important to all of us. Please don't put yourself in unnecessary danger." We all nodded vigorously in agreement when he said that.

Several days later, I was riding my bicycle around my pathway when a U.S. Army jeep pulled up in front of our house. There were two soldiers in the jeep and one hopped out. He was carrying a large manila envelope, and I could see that it was sealed on the back with wax. He saw me, ran over, and said, "Do you know where Private Grace Elaine Osborne lives?" I jumped off my bike and led him over to my apartment, and opened the door for him and followed him in. My grandmother came out of the kitchen where she had been cooking dinner. The soldier said, "Are you Private Grace Osborne?" She saluted and said that she was. The soldier handed her the envelope and asked her to sign a piece of paper he was holding; once she did so, he saluted her and hurried on his way. I could see printed on the front of the envelope the words "TOP SECRET," and additional words in longhand that I couldn't read.

My grandmother said to me, "Please turn off all the pots in the kitchen while I go up to my bedroom. I think these are my new orders, and I have to read them in private." After a few minutes, Gracie came back downstairs and told me to let the others know that she had some news, and that everyone was welcome to come over. It was as though everyone had just been sitting by their doors waiting for an invitation, because in less than ten minutes everyone was once again assembled. Gracie spoke: "I've received my orders. I'm very sorry, but the orders have been marked secret, and I can't tell you much of anything. All I can say is that I'll be traveling for a few months, with two or three other people. If I can tell you more later on, I will. I have to leave on a train going back east at noon tomorrow. Please don't think you have to see me off. I can just take a bus from here to the station."

Commie spoke up. "Gracie, don't be silly. Certainly we want to see you off, even if we can't know where you're going. And I promise we won't put on a big show like we did before." Before my grandmother could say anything, all of us enthusiastically agreed with Commie, and my grandmother relented, saying she couldn't disappoint the whole family. Even Aunt Fan, who seldom said anything at our gatherings, told her, "I feel much better about this war now. Another Osborne will help us a lot. When you get to Richmond, be sure to call my two sisters, and they'll give you a fine Southern meal." Gracie smiled and assured Fan that she would do all she could.

CHAPTER XVI

Farewell, Mr. Sato

With Gracie away on military assignment, life at Orange Grove settled back into a regular if uneasy routine. The mailman always came twice each day and would deposit letters and magazines through the mail slots in each of the four apartment doors, but I took little notice of this since I never received any mail myself, and all the magazines were for the adults. However, one day in midsummer my grandfather said to me, "Gary, here's something for you," and he handed me an envelope. I believe that was the very first piece of mail I ever received in my life. On the outside of the envelope someone had stamped "Passed by the War Relocation Authority" and had scribbled something in blue pen under the stamp, presumably the name of the person who "passed" the letter. I eagerly tore open the envelope. Inside was a single piece of lined yellow paper with a handwritten message and a small drawing on what looked like a paper napkin. This is what the message said:

> *Dear Gary. Do you remember I promised you that I would send you a postcard when I got to camp with my family? Well, I'm sorry, but they don't have any nice picture postcards here, and anyway, we're not supposed to say exactly where we are. But it really is not so bad here. It is very hot during the daytime, but it cools off at night. My*

sons George and Jimmy are here, and they are able to play baseball every day because some of us have built a nice level playing field. There isn't much else to do. The guards say that there are plans to start a school for the kids pretty soon. We'll see. Do you remember the times when I brought Jimmy with me to your place? Well, he drew a picture for you that I'll enclose with this letter. Best wishes, your friend, Jiro Sato.

I looked at the picture. In the foreground there were stick figures who were playing catch, and in the distance were some high mountains. The picture had a caption at the bottom. It said, "To my friend Gary, from Jimmy. Remember the Angels." I thought to myself that I could never draw such a fine picture, nor anything even close.

In the time before Pearl Harbor I had gotten to know several people who visited our complex almost every day: the Carnation Milk man who brought fresh milk and cream, the Helms Bakery man who delivered freshly baked bread, the "ice man" who delivered fresh ice for those of us who still had ice boxes (only Commie and Mary Margaret had an electric refrigerator), and our regular mailman. These people would always say hello to me but would never stop to talk, because they had many more houses to visit. The only visitor to our complex that had befriended me was Mr. Sato, the gardener. He would come once each week to take care of the plants in our central garden. He would park his battered old pickup truck on the street out front; the back of the truck was always overflowing with rakes, hoes and other tools. Somehow, Mr. Sato always had time to sit down with me for a few minutes, and often he would bring me a cookie or other sweet. Mr. Sato was quite small and very dark-skinned, no doubt from being in the hot Southern California sun all day, and he had a very cheerful attitude. For some reason he thought almost everything I said was funny, especially when I told him stories of my "job" with Commie, and the new home sales that I helped secure. He laughed at my stories, and sometimes asked me to tell more.

The first thing Mr. Sato would do upon arriving, after he had spoken briefly with me, was to place four canvas tarps on the ground around our circular pathway, and soon thereafter he would start filling each tarp with weeds or dead branches or other detritus. Most of the time I could not actually see Mr. Sato because he was hidden in the jungle-like garden, but I could hear him thrashing around. I was always amazed at how many weeds and pieces of trash he was able to find. Sometimes a glop of weeds and dead leaves would come sailing out from the interior of the garden and land on one of Mr. Sato's tarps. At some point Mr. Sato himself would emerge from the jungle, gather up each tarp with its weedy contents, and carry it out to his truck. Mr. Sato's final task was always to water, and he would often talk with me while he stood on the path directing the hose into the garden.

One day Mr. Sato brought his youngest son with him. His name was Jimmy. I knew he was a little older than me, but he was very friendly, just like his dad. Jimmy and I sat down on one of the garden benches, and he said to me, "Are you with the Angels or the Stars?" I hadn't the vaguest idea of what he was talking about. I'm sure he saw the confusion and ignorance in my face, because he said, "You know, we have two baseball teams here in L.A., the Angels and the Hollywood Stars. You have to be for one or the other, because the two teams are rivals." I'm sure I looked even more clueless at this point. Jimmy continued, "For me, it's all about the Angels. They have the best players and the best announcers and everything. If you don't have a team yet, you should choose the Angels." Then Jimmy said to me, "Do you know how to read a box score?" Jimmy must have thought I was the dumbest kid he had ever met, because not only did I not know the identity of our two AAA baseball teams, I didn't even know what a box score was. He said, "Is there a newspaper anywhere around here?" Finally, here was something I understood, and I replied, "Yes, I can get one…hold on a minute." I ran inside my apartment and retrieved a copy of the *Examiner* from the night before. When I gave it to Jimmy, he quickly found the sports section. He then proceeded to explain to me, with great care and detail, how to read a box score, including the names of the players, the inning-by-inning runs and hits and errors, and all the other wonderful information. On that spring day, sitting as a student to Jimmy Sato, I became a devourer of box scores, which I continue to be to this day.

I had noticed that since December of the previous year, Mr. Sato would arrive much earlier in the day. He had started to do his watering from inside the garden, where he was not visible from the street, and he brought Jimmy with him more frequently. I didn't know why until some weeks later. It was in February, not long after the Battle of Los Angeles. After Mr. Sato had finished weeding the garden and disposing of all the dead leaves, he signaled to Jimmy and me to join him in the jungle-like interior of the garden, and said, "I would like to talk to you boys for a few minutes. Let's sit on that bench." He motioned us through a slight opening in the thick foliage. I sat down next to Mr. Sato, with Jimmy on my other side. Mr. Sato said, "I wanted to tell you myself, because we've been friends now for almost a year. Jimmy and I and our family will have to leave very soon. Several days ago President Roosevelt signed an order that all Americans who have ancestors from Japan must leave California. The government is setting up concentration camps for us to live in, and the Army will take us to the camps. I've already taken George and Jimmy out of school. My wife is very afraid of what will happen to us in the camps. I wanted you to know why I will be gone very soon."

At this point he stopped talking for a few moments, and then he reached into his pocket and brought out a small wooden object. "Gary, I hope that we'll meet again, when all this horror has ended. This is a very bad time for all of us, but I have faith that things will get better…" and his voice trailed off. He put the wooden object into my hand. I saw that it was a carving of a human figure. He said, "You've made me laugh many times with your funny stories about working with Mr. Averett and going clothes shopping with Mr. Seiter. I'll always remember your stories, and while I'm away I will pray that you're still here when I get back…" When Mr. Sato said the words "when I get back," his voice cracked, and he looked away, lest I see the tears that were now coursing down his face. Jimmy and I looked at each other, but we didn't know what to say. What was in my own heart was the realization that Jimmy was the first true friend I had ever had, and now he was going away, maybe for a long time. He had taught me something I would value for the rest of my life, namely how to read a box score, and how to use that information to recreate an entire baseball game in my head.

Later in my life, I would come to know the deep misery and suffering of the tens of thousands of men, women and children incarcerated by their own government for the mere "crime" of having ancestors from Japan. I would personally visit one of the most fearsome of the camps, at Heart Mountain in the high, frigid Wyoming plateau, where winter temperatures reach 40 degrees below zero, and camp inmates had to crowd together for warmth in order to survive inside their flimsy barracks. Indeed, my wife of over 50 years is herself a survivor of that terrible place.

In fact, I never saw Jimmy or Mr. Sato again after our brief time together on Orange Grove. But for many years, the small wooden figure was among my most treasured and evocative possessions, along with the drawing that Jimmy sent me from camp. I hope Mr. Sato and his wife and sons survived their time of incarceration and that they have had good lives. Mr. Sato and his son Jimmy were the first friends to be taken from me in those awful days of the war, but they would not be the last.

CHAPTER XVII

The Lady from Virginia

The long hot summer days were especially unpleasant for me. Rosita had started spending mornings working with other Spanish-speaking women, sewing bandages, flags and other items to help with the war effort. Commie was working most days. Mary Margaret was teaching summer school. Ted was gone almost all the time. Charles was having a particularly bad time; some of his benders were lasting many days. My grandfather was spending most of his time in bed, and was mostly uncommunicative. We didn't hear from my grandmother for weeks at a time. For the first time in my life, I started spending time with the most unusual of my "family" caregivers, my aunt Fan, who had never actually taken care of me before. After an initial period of awkwardness and discomfort, I found that spending time with Fan was in fact quite enjoyable, but in an unexpected way.

Aunt Fan, whose full name was Frances Mitchell, was my grandfather's older sister. She was a rather tiny person, like most of the other Osbornes. Fan and her brother had been born in Virginia in 1873 and 1886 respectively. The Osbornes were a military family, so they had not been plantation owners; but like many Southern military families, they suffered greatly after the loss of the Civil War and the consequent disbanding of the

Confederate Army. My grandfather and his sister had moved west in their early teen years, first to Texas and then to Arizona.

Aunt Fan's precise marital history seemed to have been lost in the muddle of stories and myths she recounted to me. One of her stories involved her marrying (or being the mistress of) a U.S. senator, and she had many tales of the life of a social hostess in Washington, D.C. The story that seemed truest was that she had been the wife of a wealthy and powerful lawyer with the surname Mitchell in San Francisco in the late nineteenth century. Her only child was Theodora Mitchell. Fan never revealed what had happened to her marriage, but certainly her daughter, with whom she now lived, was real enough.

Aunt Fan had her own bedroom in Charles and Ted's apartment, where she had retreated into a fantasy world of her own creation. Her universe was filled with fancy lace gowns and ancient, yellowing photographs of her former family and friends. Fan spent her days and nights sitting at a writing desk in her dark bedroom, which was closed off from sunlight by heavy curtains. The walls of her room were covered with damask hangings and landscape paintings, and the floor was deeply carpeted. Everywhere I looked, on tabletops and shelves and old chairs, were tiny decorated boxes, pieces of jewelry, little statuettes, and small books in which Fan would occasionally write. Fan was always dressed in a floor-length gown with a frilly lace collar around her neck. Her only compromise with the reality of the day was to keep several large framed publicity photos of Ted displayed on the table nearest her writing desk.

During those difficult early days in what seemed to be a losing war, I believe I was in many ways Aunt Fan's primary point of contact with the real world. She told me her "door was always open," even though her door was in fact always closed. She could somehow sense when I was outside, and she would call out in her deep Virginia accent, "Gary Anthony, is that you out there?" When I responded, she would open her door, invite me in, pour me a glass of lemonade from the decanter on her desk, and start in on one of her incredible stories. I could listen to Aunt Fan for what seemed like hours, even though her accent was so deep that I often had to ask her to repeat words or sentences. I particularly loved when she told me stories about our family: "Gary Anthony, you listen to me now; never forget that you are an Osborne. Once upon a time we were a great family, and I believe we still are. It's just that we are in some hard times right now, but you know that your great-great-great-grandpa was Colonel William Osborne, who fought in the Revolutionary War and was a great leader of men. It was not his fault that he was a British officer, and when that war was over, he had the good sense to stay in Virginia and marry a fine Virginia girl. That is how our family started, and we have had a great leader in every war that our country has fought since then."

By "our country" Aunt Fan meant the United States of America, except for that period in the 1860s when "our country" was the Confederate States of America (CSA). I recall actually believing that Aunt Fan had somehow been present during what she called "The War Between the States," since she had so many stories of the heroism of "our boys" and the villainy of the "accursed Yankees." Aunt Fan had memorized the entire family tree, starting with the British officer Colonel Osborne. She had stories of his post-war friendship with the Virginia patriot Patrick Henry, after whom her younger brother—my grandfather—had been named. Fan always delighted in showing me her now yellowed copy of Patrick Henry's famous "Give Me Liberty or Give me Death" speech to the Virginia legislature. She would quote long passages of the speech from heart, accompanied by her own dramatic pauses and cries. For me, my aunt Fan actually became the Great Patriot himself, which is perhaps what she intended. During such times I realized that Ted took after her mother, at least with respect to theatricality.

Aunt Fan's stories were enlivened for me because she always produced some kind of prop for me to handle or play with. When she told stories of the War Between the States, she might hand me some CSA money, with President Jefferson Davis's face where Washington's might appear on "Yankee money." Or if she was telling me about the exploits of some Osborne in the Spanish-American War, she would let me hold an old necklace, which she explained was captured during a campaign in the mountains of Cuba. Aunt Fan must have had drawers and drawers of souvenirs—real or imagined, I never knew—from our family's supposed military exploits. I recall that she seemed disappointed that her younger brother, Patrick Henry Osborne, had never been a military hero, but she forgave him because Patrick's only son, William Lloyd, had become an Army officer and was serving under the command of General Douglas MacArthur, who for some reason she always described as "that great Southern general."

Aunt Fan's supply of Confederate paraphernalia seemed endless, but there was one sacred object that I never saw. One day Fan said to me, "I am the guardian of the most sacred object that our family owns, which is the official CSA officer's pistol that was carried throughout the war by Colonel Osborne. Together with the pistol is the diary that Colonel Osborne kept throughout that war, when he fought with the Army of Northern Virginia under the command of the great General Lee himself. The pistol is kept in a locked cabinet, which is hidden in this very room. The only two keys are held by me and your uncle Lloyd." To this very day, I sometimes find myself transported back to Aunt Fan's darkened bedroom, where I am once again listening to her vivid stories of the Old South, and of my forebears' exploits during the great War Between the States.

The only negative part of my visits with Aunt Fan was a little Pekingese dog whom I found to be very ugly and ill-tempered. This unpleasant animal spent most of his waking hours nestled on Fan's lap. Whenever I entered Fan's bedroom, the dog would look at me with obvious suspicion and hostility, made worse by his large protuberant eyes. Even when Fan moved away from her desk to locate some object she wanted to use to illustrate one of her stories, she managed to use one hand to keep the dog close against her body. Fan appeared to be unaware of the ill feelings the dog had for me, or the fact that I found the animal quite disgusting. The dog did not fit my idea of what a canine should be, active and friendly and a good companion for a young boy. Often when I visited Fan, she would ask me to feed the animal table scraps she had saved from previous meals and placed in specially marked containers in Charles' icebox. The scraps had been pre-cut into bite-sized chunks for the dog, so I didn't have to do any cutting or other preparation. Still, I didn't relish handling the cold meats, so I would quickly drop them into the dog's dish and take it into Fan's room, at which Fan would announce to the dog, "Oh, look what Gary Anthony has brought you, some very nice dinner. Wouldn't you like to have some dinner now?" She would then slip the dog off her lap, presuming that he would head for his food dish, but in fact he would merely stand on the carpet glaring at me with his big watery Pekingese eyes. There was much unspoken hostility exchanged between the small, furry, pug-nosed animal and me.

In future years, after I had left the Orange Grove complex, I returned as often as possible to visit with Aunt Fan. She lived to be close to 100 years old. Amazingly, she always had new stories and new "family secrets" to tell me. She never seemed to age or change in any way, even into her ninth decade. In later years I came to realize that Fan's stories of the Old South were part of a process of romanticizing Southern history, ignoring the inhuman horrors of slavery, denying its central role in causing the Civil War, and glossing over the implementation of Jim Crow throughout the Old Confederacy after the war. But as a child, all this was in my future, and Fan's stories still held my fullest attention. However, I never did see what Fan considered our family's most valuable treasure, Colonel Osborne's CSA pistol from the War Between the States.

CHAPTER XVIII

Patrick Henry Osborne

My relationship with my grandfather was unusual and mysterious. It was not uncommon for me to go three or four days without saying a single word to him, and hearing only silence in return. Despite his small stature and thin body, when I was in his presence I had a distinct feeling of security and safety, manifested by a physical sense of warmth. I recall waking up on cold winter mornings (there was no heat in my little upstairs bedroom), and hurrying down to our living room, where my grandfather spent almost all his waking hours. On seeing my grandfather sitting in his favorite easy chair, encased in the multicolored quilt he always wore around his narrow shoulders, the cold would leave my shivering body. I remember that I always looked directly into his face and that he always looked back at me with the slightest flicker of a smile. For me this was powerfully reassuring.

All my life I have wondered about the mysterious communication that took place so wordlessly between my grandfather and me. It is only in the writing of this memoir that I have come to understand the origin of my feelings for my grandfather, and his for me. Perhaps you, astute reader, have already put two and two together, but it has taken me over 70 years to see a clear picture. As I mentioned previously, my mother divorced my father when I was just an infant. She moved back in with her parents at a time when my grandmother was already working full time and my grandfather, for whatever mental or physical reason, was "at home." It must have been decided that the best strategy for the family's future was for my mother to go work as a teacher and for me to be cared for by my grandparents. I now understand that the "mysterious" bond that I felt when we lived in our Orange Grove apartment was the result of hundreds of days and thousands of hours of being carried around, spoken to, and soothed by my grandfather. As I now hold my own grandsons in my arms, so must my own grandfather have done with me, except in his case on a daily basis. So when I would come downstairs on cold mornings, and feel warmth in seeing my grandfather, it was the product of his having cared for me during those years before I was able to speak, and before my conscious memory had engaged.

My grandfather's full name was Patrick Henry Osborne. He told me once that he had struggled his whole life trying to live up to the legacy of his namesake, and that it was very hard because the original Patrick Henry had been a firebrand, a ferocious debater, and a leader of men, whereas my grandfather was by nature quiet, thoughtful, serious and self-effacing. My grandfather apparently knew everything there was to know about the "give me liberty or give me death" Virginia patriot, and could recite parts of his more famous speeches. He also considered himself, like Patrick Henry before him, to be first and foremost a Virginian. When he and his sister Fan spent time together, they would often talk about people and places unknown to the rest of us, perhaps from their youths spent in Richmond and Fredericksburg. Between the two of them, they could name Osbornes from every generation since the Revolutionary War.

My grandfather had a special fondness for accurately measuring things. This skill had become his vocation when he started doing instrumentation work for mining companies in Arizona. It was essential for the safety of underground miners that air quality be accurately measured, and the profitability of the company depended on precise measurement of the purity of the mined ore. When my grandfather moved his family to Huntington Beach, California, after the closure of the mines in Arizona, he continued his work as an instrument-based recorder of information, now for the Union Oil Company.

At some point, in the mid- to late-1930s, something happened that ended my grandfather's working life. My grandmother's explanation was that he had a stroke. In later years I wondered if he had suffered some kind of emotional collapse or depression, perhaps brought on by the family's economic decline during the Great Depression. I will never know for sure, but what I do know is that my grandfather spent most of his days and evenings sitting in his chair, either reading one of the daily newspapers we received, or simply staring off into space. Under my grandmother's watchful eye, he always maintained an outward appearance of dignity; and after her departure to take Lloyd's place in the Army, he continued to maintain his appearance. Fortunately for both of us, my grandmother made sure that my grandfather and I would be well-fed, so all our meals were brought in, usually by Rosita and sometimes by Mary Margaret. These women also cleaned the dishes, washed our clothes, and in general tried to fill my grandmother's role.

Although in my memory there was a lot of silence in our apartment after my grandmother went off to war, sometimes my grandfather would comment favorably on a picture I had drawn, and he would always thank me if I brought him the newspaper or carried in the mail (which in those days was delivered twice a day). Almost every evening we would listen to the radio, usually to comedies such as Jack Benny, Fred Allen, or Burns & Allen, but also to dramatizations. And at 8:00 p.m. every night during the cold months, together with thousands of other Southern Californians, we would hear Floyd D. Young's resonant baritone voice saying, "Good evening, this is Floyd D. Young at KFI Los Angeles, with tonight's frost warnings." It was surprising that this nightly institution was so hugely popular, because it merely involved Mr. Young repeating the same list of citrus-growing towns in Los Angeles and Orange Counties and their predicted low temperatures: "Anaheim, 28; Azusa, 27; Cucamonga, 30; Corona, 26," and so forth for several minutes. But there was something poetic, mesmerizing, hypnotic about Floyd Young's voice, and the rich litany of the place names of so many strange, unknown towns. The purpose of the nightly frost warnings was so that citrus farmers would be alerted if they needed to light the thousands of smudge pots that produced thick, warm smoke all night to keep the orange trees from freezing. If the temperature was going to be below freezing on a particular night, my grandfather would say "Brrrrrr," and pull his lap blanket closer to his thin body.

Each week there was a major exception to my grandfather's usual silence, and that involved a Saturday night ritual that he treasured and always shared with me. This was the live radio broadcast of the Grand Ole Opry from Nashville, Tennessee. The radio feeds were always scratchy, and frequently interrupted by static, but it made no difference to my grandfather. He made sure he and I were sitting comfortably in front of the five-foot-high radio that dominated our living room. He gave strict instructions to the rest of our family that we were not to be disturbed for the full hour of the Opry broadcast. I later learned that many Southerners who shared my grandfather's aristocratic attitudes did not particularly like what was sometimes referred to as "hillbilly music." But my grandfather, who as far as I know was not otherwise musically inclined, had made a study of Opry-style music, and after most

Opry broadcasts he would tell me stories about the origins of the music. He knew, for instance, that one of the main sources of country music was from his own state of Virginia, and he was very familiar with the "Bristol Sessions," where the first recordings were made of the Carter Family in Bristol, a town on the Virginia/Tennessee border. He was always very pleased when the Carter Family appeared on the Opry, and he loved the main host, the great singer and songwriter Roy Acuff.

My grandfather never used the term "hillbilly" to refer to the music he and I listened to every Saturday night. Rather, he referred to it as "Scotch-Irish," with a direct connection to the origins of "his people" (and therefore mine also). For many years I thought of my own heritage as Irish, focusing on the "Irish" of the Scotch-Irish appellation. Only much later did I learn the true history of the Scotch-Irish (or "Scots-Irish") people, who had been forced off their traditional lands in Scotland and spent some years or generations in Northern Ireland without ever becoming religiously or culturally "Irish." These people had then immigrated to the United States and settled in the Appalachian mountains of western Virginia, North Carolina and Tennessee, where their descendants still live today. My grandfather told me that certain Opry songs had come directly from Glasgow or Aberdeen but with updated words to reflect their new American identity.

I was always amazed at how much my grandfather knew about the Opry music and the performers and their different styles. His favorite genre was what is now known as "country folk," represented more recently by singers like Loretta Lynn and Emmylou Harris. He also liked what he called "Kentucky" music, which later became bluegrass. He was not nearly as fond of what he called "redneck" and "honkytonk" music, which he told me came from "nasty places like Mississippi." In fact, the only time my generally placid and dignified grandfather became exercised was when he spoke of "rednecks" and "hicks." He had a visceral dislike for Southerners who did not share his cultural attitudes. He would often mention the names of "the Great Virginians" like Washington, Jefferson and Madison, and of course the Lee family, and Patrick Henry himself. Much of my education about my family's heritage and my grandfather's background came from the stories he told me after Opry broadcasts.

As news of American defeats and losses in the war came into our lives, I think it caused the most pain to my grandfather. Others in our family, like my grandmother and Commie and Rosita, were able to participate actively in the "war effort," but my grandfather's inability to do anything overtly helpful must have been very hard on him. When he read stories in the paper about continued misery and death in places like the Philippines and Guadalcanal, I would see him shake his head, and sometimes whisper things that I could not make out. Unfortunately, as the war progressed and Gracie's absences became more prolonged, my grandfather seemed to become more and more detached from reality. He even pulled out his old rifle, which I hadn't even known he possessed, and sometimes held it beside himself while he sat in his chair, as if for protection. My extended family made certain that the gun was never loaded.

CHAPTER XIX

The Home Front, 1942

In the evenings I often asked Mary Margaret to help me learn to read more fluently, so I could better understand what was happening in the world and the progress of the war. In those days we received three or four different newspapers, including the mainstay *L.A. Times*, the super right-wing *L.A. Examiner*, and the afternoon Hearst paper, the *Herald Express*. The only person who read the *Examiner* was my grandfather, who must have found its politics to his liking. Someone had given me a globe for a previous birthday, and I learned to find the locations of battles that were raging in Asia, Europe, and now even in Africa. I had also inherited my uncle Lloyd's old *World Atlas*, and I enjoyed looking up cities and rivers and deserts that were mentioned in the news, even though some of the country names had changed.

The news was still mostly bad: the Japanese conquest of Asia continued apace, and no one seemed able to stop the advance of the Imperial forces. The news from Europe and North Africa was also terrible. It appeared that a Nazi invasion of England was only a matter of time. I soon discovered that morale in my neighborhood was very low. One morning Commie came over to me and said, "Gary, I'm sorry that we haven't been able to go out together recently to sell houses. I think you must know that I'm devoting almost all my time to the Civil Defense. Yesterday I was trying to calm down a family over on Ogden Street, and one of their kids started screaming hysterically about the bombings and how we were all going to die, and it suddenly occurred to me that you could be a big help to me in dealing with problems like that. So, if you are willing, I'd like to ask you to start accompanying me on my rounds." I felt a thrill in being asked to do something specific to help the war effort. Of course I told Commie that I would do whatever I could.

I was aware that Commie had been a "block captain" with the Civil Defense since a few weeks after Pearl Harbor, because he wore an armband with "CD" on it. He was always rushing off to meetings and training sessions, but if I ever asked him what he was doing, he would respond, "I can't really talk about it, because it's supposed to be top secret." As I soon discovered, Civil Defense duties were not in fact confidential, but Commie liked to pretend that he was doing something very, very important, and that secrecy was part of his job. I think his initial idea about Civil Defense was that he would be exposing spy rings and the like. Although the day-to-day responsibilities were more pedestrian, what he was doing was indeed important, but for quite different reasons than he knew.

The morning after Commie had invited me to accompany him on his rounds, he told me he had to go to a block captain meeting, and as soon as he returned he would give me my own training. True to his word, as soon as he had returned from his meeting, he took me to his apartment and told me, "Gary, there are some things about the Civil Defense that I can't tell you, but I do want you to know as much as possible so that you can help me. There are several important things that we need to do. First is to make sure that everyone, and I do mean everyone, observes the blackouts. There are some people in our neighborhood, especially down on Pickford Street, who don't fully cooperate. They're careless about displaying lights, and believe me, that's all the Japanese bombers need to blast us to smithereens." Blackouts had started even before Pearl Harbor, but had not been very effective until the horrible destruction of the American fleet and loss of so many young lives forced us to face reality. Once people were aware of the true power of the Japanese naval and air forces, they had taken the blackout orders much more seriously. However, after the debacle of the Battle of Los Angeles, and no sightings of Japanese ships or planes in the ensuing weeks and months, the public resolve began to weaken. As block captain, Commie saw it as his main job to ensure that there were no lighted targets for the bombers, if and when they arrived. He said to me, "With two of us, we can be even more thorough in locating lights. Once we do, it will be up to me to correct the situation."

Commie continued, "After making sure that blackouts are effective, our next priorities are to ensure that rationing is being enforced, and that no one is doing any 'black market' stuff." Commie explained to me that many food items and other daily supplies were now in short supply and therefore rationed, and some unscrupulous and greedy people were now trying to sell these items illegally. If we found anyone doing that, we would immediately report them to the police.

Commie's other CD responsibilities included encouraging people to plant "Victory Gardens" and to save grease and fat. Commie was assiduous about the Victory Gardens. The Civil Defense had given him seed packets and planting instructions; it was his goal that every single house or apartment complex in our neighborhood would have its own Victory Garden. Commie felt that to be effective, the war effort needed to involve people of all ages, and that children could play important roles such as helping grow vegetables. In fact, shortly after Commie started taking me on his rounds, the CD authorities had started a "Youth Auxiliary" program, and I now had my own official armband and plastic helmet as I accompanied Commie around the neighborhood. It became my role to teach other kids how to plant certain vegetables—carrots were my specialty, as they were quite easy to grow—and how to weed without uprooting the food plants. This new role of mine was in a sense ironic, because I had never lived on a farm and had no prior planting experience, whereas some of the other kids I was "teaching" had actually been raised on farms and were much more comfortable than I was working the soil. It must have been the sense of authority conveyed by my little CD armband and plastic helmet that made the other kids listen politely, as I "taught" them how to tend their Victory Gardens.

CHAPTER XX

A Visit from Gracie

On a warm Sunday afternoon in early May, I was circling the courtyard on my bike, hoping that Commie would come out and ask me to accompany him on his Civil Defense rounds, when a dark green U.S. Army sedan pulled up in front of our complex. I was close to the street and could only see the driver and an officer in the back seat. The driver, who looked to me like a teenager but wore an Army uniform, got out, came around to the right rear door, and opened it. A middle-aged officer emerged, soon followed by my own grandmother, also in uniform. I had not seen my grandmother in what seemed like a very long time, and I burst out in uncontrollable tears and sobbing. My grandmother immediately took me into her arms, gave me a big hug, and said, "I'm so happy to see you too, but now you have to gather everyone into our apartment. I only have a few minutes to spend here, and I want to tell you all a few things."

I scurried around, trying to rouse everyone, but only Commie, Mary Margaret, Rosita, Charles, Fan and my grandfather were at home. When we were all seated in our living room, my grandmother addressed us. "I would like you all to meet Captain Phillips, who is my immediate superior officer." These words were very ironic, since it was obvious that Gracie was in fact in charge, and that Captain Phillips' role was to accompany Gracie and help her accomplish whatever she was assigned to do. To me, my grandmother seemed like a totally different person than she had been before the war; now she was so strong, so sure of herself, so confident. Certainly she was still my grandmother, my primary caregiver, the person to whom I looked when I needed support the most. But she had changed in important ways. I had the feeling she could get her way with anyone on any subject. This is what she said to us:

"First, I'm sorry that I haven't been in touch, but Captain Phillips and I have been traveling almost all the time, to many unusual places. I can't tell you very much about what I've been doing, but I can tell you this: we are now sure that women will play an extremely important role in our difficult struggles over the next months and years. I'm not talking about helping on 'the home front' as wives and mothers. I'm talking about filling urgent and vital military roles that women have never done before. At this very moment, all of us—men and women, soldiers and civilians—are embarked on the most difficult task this nation has ever faced. We have just entered bloody combat in dozens of places most of us have never heard of but will be reading about in coming weeks, places like New Guinea and the Solomon Islands. Many lives will be lost, including many of our WAACs, like the ones I trained with in Des Moines, and subsequent groups that proved themselves just as we did. We've shown our strength and toughness in training, and already some of my closest pals are about to launch combat nursing stations where beachheads have been opened. As you know, I myself wanted to be close to the front just as Lloyd was, but my senior officers feel I can be most effective in meeting with Army and Marines and Navy officers and ensuring they understand what women's roles will—and must—be."

With those words, my grandmother signaled to Captain Phillips, and they prepared to leave. Gracie then said, "I'm absolutely counting on all of you to take care of my beloved Gary. I'd remain here if I could, but I have an important a job to do, and I do it knowing that you all support me, and that you will give this boy—this young man—everything he needs." At this point she took me into her arms again, causing me to break out in convulsive sobs once more. Before any one of us could say anything else, my grandmother and her "senior officer" were out the door and driving off. For a while no one spoke; we had been so mesmerized by the power and drama of Gracie's words, and the aura of her strength. I could never have imagined that my own grandmother could speak with such great eloquence.

After some minutes, Mary Margaret stood up and said, "All of us need to tell the others what Gracie told us, and we need to do our jobs as best we can." When the others had left, I sat for a long time by myself, trying to imagine what it would be like to actually experience the kind of war about which my grandmother had spoken, and what her WAAC buddies would be living through. I also wondered when I would see my grandmother again. If I had known what would soon transpire, my heart would have been in my throat.

CHAPTER XXI

A New Dawn

During the late summer of 1942, I was spending almost every evening accompanying Commie on his rounds, which had expanded to include three additional blocks of territory that he had taken over from less eager Civil Defense men. Recent news from the front was discouraging, and Commie and I despaired at the low morale in our neighborhood; I knew that some people, like Mrs. O'Grady, had packed up and left L.A. altogether, fearing that an invasion was imminent. Adding to the near-hysteria were constant stories about the savagery of Japanese treatment of civilians in areas they had captured. News of the brutal Bataan Death March had trickled out via the "bamboo newswire" (news sent from missionaries and local officials via secret shortwave radios in the Philippines, Malaya, and the Dutch East Indies).

However, in early fall, and seemingly overnight, we noticed a significant change in attitude as we were doing our rounds, almost as if some huge hidden button had been pushed. It was as though everyone had decided they had had enough defeatism and fear, and it was now time to win the war.

In my memory, the change from discouragement and fear to optimism and hope is associated with an event that had little to do with the actual war. It happened on one of those rare L.A. days when the air is crystalline, and I could clearly see from the Santa Monica Mountains in the west all the way to the San Gabriel Mountains in the east, the white top of Mt. Baldy shining with reflected splendor. I remember that I was sitting on my bike enjoying the view, when unexpectedly, Mr. Seiter's limousine pulled up. As usual, the liveried driver got out and opened the rear passenger door. Out jumped a tall and very beautiful woman, whom I recognized as a movie star since I had seen her likeness on billboards. Just as she emerged into the sunshine, I heard a joyous shriek behind me. Ted, who had come out of her apartment, ran up to the woman and threw her arms around her. The two looked just like high school best friends who were seeing each other for the first time after a summer apart. They jumped up and down, speaking quickly in Spanish and English, laughing and poking each other playfully. Finally Ted pointed over her shoulder and they headed, arm in arm, toward Ted and Charles' apartment.

The woman was Rita Hayworth. Ted had often spoken about her. The two had roomed together when they both danced in Tijuana, Rita as "Rita Cansino" and Ted as "Conchita Mitchell." Ted told me they often spoke on the phone but rarely got to see each other face-to-face due to being on location. Now, of course, Rita was one of the biggest stars in Hollywood. Her famous negligee photo would soon become one of the most widely seen "cheesecake" pictures in Army camps and on Navy ships throughout the world. Ted and Rita were almost exactly the same height, and both moved with the grace and confidence of professional dancer athletes. Ted later told me that Rita was co-starring with Fred Astaire in Mr. Seiter's current film, and that Rita confided she had "never worked harder in her f***ing life" (Ted was the only one in our family who used swear words). Due to Fred Astaire's famous "rehearse all day and night" habits, Rita was doing the best work of her life. In fact, for a time after the release of the film, Rita became Mr. Astaire's most highly regarded partner.

So entranced was I, watching Ted and Rita acting like excited girls, I had not noticed Mr. Seiter get out of his limo. Unexpectedly, he was now standing next to me. He said, "I called Charles this morning and asked him to tell Ted that I'd be bringing Rita by, so she could get ready. I also told Charles that he, you and I should talk for a few minutes. I'll go get him and we'll sit on the little bench in your garden." I had noticed before that Mr. Seiter had a way of seeming to suggest that you take a particular action, but phrasing it so you didn't actually have any choice. Within a few minutes he had managed to locate Charles, and the two of them came out of Charles' apartment together. I knew that Charles was in the midst of a recovery phase, which now often took four or more days. As Charles emerged into the clear bright L.A. sunshine, he seemed momentarily blinded, but Mr. Seiter guided him to the bench at the rear of our garden (which was now completely overgrown and jungle-like, having gone without the tender care of Mr. Sato for many months). I had always known that Mr. Seiter was the fitter and handsomer of the brothers, but this time it was even more dramatically evident. Mr. Seiter was dressed impeccably, with a lovely maroon tie and cream-colored vest under a grey suit. Charles had at least shaved, but he still looked unkempt and rumpled.

Mr. Seiter sat on one side of me, with Charles on the other. Mr. Seiter cut right to the chase. "Today I'm more optimistic than I've been in a long time—since before Pearl Harbor, as a matter of fact. A lot of us in Hollywood have decided we can play a huge role in the war effort, and we're trying to get everybody on board. My boss, Mr. Cohn, who runs Columbia Studios, and who—just between us—can be a bit of a skinflint, said he wanted me to make the biggest and happiest musical that money can buy, so people can get their minds off all the fighting and dying. He gave me a blank check. Well, the film's almost done, and it cost a lot of money, but I think it'll do the job. I have Fred Astaire and Rita Hayworth, and they're sensational. I got Jerry Kern to write the music. Of course, he's a genius. Johnny Mercer is working with me and Jerry on the lyrics, and we have Cugat's orchestra. You'll see the film pretty soon—I'll arrange for you two and Ted to be at the premiere.

"But here's what I really want to talk to you about. Gary, Charles, I've been taking my son Christopher with me on location for some of the shooting for this film. And I've realized that what makes me happiest is to be able to spend time with my son, and for him to see what I do. Charles, my beloved brother, I so much want you to have this same experience. I've been asked by Harry Cohn and the Warner boys to lead a Hollywood effort to do what we do best, namely make money. But this time the money we make will go directly to the war effort. Charles, Gary"—here Mr. Seiter became very serious—"we absolutely have to win this war. It's a matter of survival, a matter of life as we know it. This may be the most important thing any of us will ever do. And I'm going to make sure that my son is with me and sees what I do. Charles"—Mr. Seiter took Charles' hand in his—"I want you and Gary to be at my side, along with my son Christopher. We have an enormous job ahead of us. We need to raise literally millions of dollars. We need to organize tours to our military bases and to where our boys are fighting. We need to build up the USO. Los Angeles is now the embarkation point for thousands of young men going off to fight in the Pacific. Before they board their ships, I want them to meet the stars they idolize, like Duke Wayne and Betty Grable and Crosby and Hope and, of course, Rita, so they know that America is behind them. There's so much work for us to do, and I want both of you to be with me."

I had known how persuasive Mr. Seiter could be; and at that moment, sitting on our little bench, with Rita Hayworth and Ted still whooping and laughing from inside Ted's apartment, I would have followed Mr. Seiter anywhere. Charles was nodding affirmatively to whatever his older brother said, and saying things like, "Of course, Bill, whatever we can do," but I could tell that Charles was not fully absorbing the implications of his brother's plans. In a sense I actually knew Charles better than his brother did at this time, because I saw Charles at both his highs, when he was truly William Seiter's brother, and at his lows when he was coming off a bender, hardly able to walk or speak. I also knew that Mr. Seiter's vision of Charles and Ted and me as a family unit, in the model of himself, Marian and Christopher, was perhaps beyond Charles' capacity to pull off. At that moment I hoped it was possible, but even at my young age I had my doubts.

Following our conversation, Mr. Seiter quickly made the rounds of our four apartments, saying positive, uplifting words to those who were home, especially Rosita and my grandfather. He then walked quickly back to Ted and Charles' apartment, retrieved a reluctant Rita Hayworth, and within a minute or two they were back in their limo and taking off.

That evening we had a family meeting, this time led by Ted, which was unusual. The only family members not present were my grandfather and Aunt Fan, who were both in their own worlds at this point. Ted thanked those of us in attendance and explained how Mr. Seiter and Rita Hayworth had visited, that Rita wanted Ted to work with her on a war bond project, and that Mr. Seiter had also recruited Charles and me. Ted said, "I haven't followed the war effort very closely, but I understand that our country is finally getting mobilized. I think each and every one of us can do something important. We shouldn't just leave it to Gracie."

At this point Commie said, "Ted's right. Things are changing in a big way. After Pearl Harbor it seemed that the Japanese won every battle, and the same was true with the Nazis in Europe. But recently the government announced that we had success in one of the biggest naval battles in our history, at Midway, north of Hawaii. The Japanese thought they were finishing what they started at Pearl Harbor by destroying the rest of our fleet, but just the opposite happened. We won the Battle of Midway, and we sunk a very important part of the Japanese fleet. Now Hawaii is safe. And Hawaii will be the stopping-off point for thousands of American sailors and Marines and Army soldiers who will attack Japanese occupation forces all over the Pacific. The tide of the war has changed. The morale of people right here in Los Angeles has also changed." Commie looked around the room and continued, "So Ted is right. Each of us has a role to play, and each of us should dedicate ourselves, right here and now, to being part of the victory ahead."

Homer said, "You all know that Rosita has been working many hours with the Spanish-speaking community, and I would like to join Charles in his Civil Defense work." Mary Margaret said she would increase her hours with the Red Cross. Charles said something vague about helping out his brother, but it was clear he was still in recovery and anxious to get back to bed. Finally Ted said, "This is a new day. Let us be inspired by the example Gracie's setting for all of us. She's dedicated every waking hour to helping our country, and she's putting her life on the line. Let us also be inspired by the memory of Lloyd, whom we all loved so much."

As the meeting was breaking up, Commie took me aside and told me, "You know we haven't been selling any houses lately, but that's about to change. There are thousands of workers coming to Los Angeles right now, because we're the nation's biggest aircraft manufacturer. You know those big companies over in Santa

Monica, North American and Boeing, and Lockheed over in Burbank and Northrup down near Inglewood? They're going on 24-hour shifts, because they have huge backlogs of planes to make. This war may be won in the air, and most of the Allied planes will be made right here in L.A. All these new workers need places to live. Starting tomorrow, you and I are going to start selling houses again."

By this time my head was spinning. I was going to renew my role as Commie's "perfect young man" for the wives of homebuyers. I was going to join Charles and Ted in raising money from Hollywood stars, and I was going to work evenings and nights with the Civil Defense. It all sounded exciting, but also confusing. I set my mind to doing the best I could with each of my jobs. But I was unprepared for perhaps the most momentous day of my life.

CHAPTER XXII

Once More Unto the Breach

It was late in the evening, well after my bedtime. The phone downstairs in the kitchen was ringing off the hook and no one was answering it. In those days it was highly unusual for the phone to ring after 9:00 p.m. I turned on the light in my bedroom and went downstairs. I knocked on my grandfather's bedroom door, but got no answer. Then I noticed that the front door was ajar. I peeked out, and my grandfather was sitting in a chair on the landing, fast asleep, with his rifle across his lap. The phone was still ringing. I went into the kitchen, picked up the receiver and said, "Hello?"

The voice at the other end said, "This is the *L.A. Times* calling. Is your mother or father home?" I said no, and that my grandfather was unable to come to the phone. The person asked if this was the home of Captain William Osborne, and I told him it was. The man then said, "You're on Orange Grove, just south of Pico, right? I'll be there in 15 minutes." Before I could respond, the man hung up.

I ran over to Commie's apartment and pounded on the door, and in a few moments Mary Margaret opened it. I told her about the phone call. She instructed me to rouse Rosita, and within a few minutes everyone except Fan had arrived in my front room, all still in their robes or pajamas. A few minutes later, five strangers, two with cameras, pulled up on the street and hurried towards our complex. The commotion had awakened my grandfather, who was now sitting in a chair in the living room, looking dazed and confused, but still holding his rifle. Within a few seconds the strangers had entered and were looking around the room, noticing the disparity in our ages and apparel. One of the men said, "We're sorry to disturb you at this ungodly hour, but when you hear our news, I think you'll understand. Less than an hour ago we received a report directly from our reporter based at General MacArthur's headquarters in Australia. The report was very brief, and this is exactly what it said."

He read from a printed sheet: "General MacArthur has reported that the first American soldiers to escape from the Bataan Death March have just landed on the north coast of Australia. One is an infantry captain from Los Angeles named Osborne. The other is a fighter pilot from Georgia named Gause. The Australian Air Force is flying them to meet with General MacArthur and his staff. This is extremely important news, because we thought no one had survived or avoided capture by the Japanese." The *Times* reporter continued, "I assume you all are Captain Osborne's family. I thought you would want to hear this news."

Speechless. Our mouths were hanging open. Could it be true? Could Lloyd be alive? Could our most secret prayers have somehow been answered? The room was silent for what seemed an eternity. Finally, the *Times* reporter said, "Could I get your names, please?" Ted was the first to recover enough to respond and said, "This gentleman"—pointing to my grandfather—"is Lloyd's father; his name is Patrick Henry Osborne. This is Patrick's sister and her name is Frances, and I'm her daughter, Theodora. This is my husband, Charles Seiter. Here are our closest friends, who know Lloyd very well—Commodore Perry Averett and his wife Mary Margaret—and over here are Homer and Rosita

Burt. This young man is Lloyd's nephew, Gary. We all assumed Lloyd was dead. His mother, Grace, has joined the United States Army to take his place, and she's somewhere on assignment." I was amazed at how Ted was able to be such an eloquent spokeswoman for our family. We were thankful that she took charge at this time of our amazement and surprise.

The reporters stayed only a few minutes. The photographers took individual pictures of all of us, and several group pictures. One of the reporters tried to interview my grandfather, but to no avail. My grandfather seemed to be living in another world, and had not yet absorbed that his "worst day forever" had apparently been transformed.

The next few days were a whirlwind of activity. Reporters from various newspapers, radio stations, and news magazines were in our complex at all hours. Since there was no further news from Australia about the details of Lloyd's situation, the reporters wrote numerous stories about those of us in his "family" in order to fill the pages. Several stories falsely described Charles as an executive in the film industry, probably confusing him with his brother. Ted was invariably described as a successful actress or, in one story, as Rita Hayworth's sister. Commie was described as a "major Southern California real estate magnate." In one story I was described as "the founder of the Youth Auxiliary of the Civil Defense." In the evenings, different members of our family would read these stories out loud to one another and laugh at the crazy exaggerations and false statements. This was my first real exposure to the fact that not everything printed in a newspaper is the truth.

We were expecting that the Army would send someone over to brief us soon, but it took several days, and even then, the Army captain who came to our complex told us that he had little new information, but did confirm that Lloyd was safe and well. We were greatly relieved by his visit, because it was hard to believe that the news about Lloyd could actually be true. Since the beginning of the war, there had been many hopeful news stories that turned out to be untrue, and even some reports of U.S. victories that had never happened. The Army captain explained to us that General MacArthur's command had just moved from Melbourne to Brisbane in the far north of Australia, and that it was difficult to get news from there. We soon learned that the possibility of a Japanese invasion of Australia was being taken very seriously, especially since the Japanese had invaded New Guinea, only a few hundred miles off Australia's coastline. Plans were underway for U.S. and Australian counterattacks on New Britain and other islands occupied by the Japanese. The Battle for Guadalcanal in the Solomon Islands, which would be one of the bloodiest and most difficult battles in American military history, had commenced, and its outcome was still unknown. All these military efforts were being coordinated by General MacArthur as Supreme Allied Commander in the Southwest Pacific.

More than a week after the night we were awakened by the journalists, a U.S. Army car pulled up to our house. An Army colonel and a lieutenant quickly got out. I recognized the lieutenant from a previous visit, and he smiled at me as he guided the colonel to my apartment door. I quickly gathered whoever was home. The colonel told us, "I have rather amazing news about Captain Osborne. As you know, at the time of the Japanese attack on the Philippines, he was in command of a battalion of American and Filipino troops. They fought valiantly, but were overwhelmed by superior numbers. Virtually all of our troops were either killed or captured. Those who were captured were forced into the Bataan Death March, where many more died. We know there were mass executions of our officers. Somehow, Captain Osborne managed to escape. For several months he went from village to village, where he was sheltered and protected by the local people. Finally he heard about another American who had escaped, and the two of them managed to find each other. The other man was an Army fighter pilot, Captain Damon Gause.

"The two of them decided to try to escape the Philippines entirely. They were told that the Japanese had captured all of the Philippine islands, and more islands to the south almost all the way to Australia, but that Australia was still in Allied hands. Somehow they managed to find a boat. They pretended to be Filipino fishermen, and they set sail for the south. For many weeks they sailed from island to island, all Japanese held, but managed to avoid being captured. Several times Japanese fighter plans tried to sink their boat, but they had a Japanese flag, which they waved. Miraculously, they finally managed to reach the north coast of Australia. Of course, Captains Osborne and Gause now have invaluable information about Japanese troop locations and the placement of new airbases. They're among the first men to escape the Philippines and live to tell about it. They're great heroes, and General MacArthur has already conferred the highest medal on both of them, the Distinguished Service Cross. As we speak, they're still being debriefed by our senior intelligence officers in General MacArthur's headquarters. When possible, they will return to the U.S. to be reunited with their families."

We were all thinking the same thing, and Commie spoke the words: "Has Lloyd's mother been informed?"

The lieutenant responded, "Yes, Private Osborne has been notified, and I'm sure she'll be here with all of you when Captain Osborne returns. I wish I knew when that will be, but General MacArthur's headquarters won't say."

It's hard to describe the level of excitement and tension of the next few weeks. In these early days of the Pacific War, the news was still mostly bad, with high casualty lists, grim news of Japanese atrocities, more territory lost on the Asian mainland, and even a successful Japanese invasion and subsequent occupation of part of Alaska. The prospect of a return to U.S. soil by two flesh-and-blood heroes was major news nationwide, and the fact that one of the two had gone to UCLA was a source of great pride for Southern California.

* * *

Finally, the great day came. All our little family was picked up by U.S. Army cars, and we were driven to an airbase near Santa Monica. We were escorted to a VIP section on the field, where we were seated. Just in front of our section was a podium and about ten chairs, facing us. The press was confined to a section just behind where we were sitting. After a short wait, another Army car pulled up in front of our seats, and out climbed two generals, followed by my grandmother. We had not seen her for at least a month, nor had we seen her since we received the news that Lloyd was alive. My grandmother said something to one of the generals, then came over to us and hugged each one. She took my grandfather's hand and guided him to a seat behind the podium, and sat down with him on one side and the two generals on the other. After a few more minutes we saw a large U.S. Army Air Corps airplane in the distance. It landed and taxied over to near where we were seated. When the engines stopped, access stairs were wheeled over to the plane, and the passenger door was opened from inside. A number of high-ranking Army officers and some Navy and Marine officers emerged. My heart was in my throat, and I could barely contain my excitement. There was a pause after all the officers had descended to the ground, and then, silhouetted in the doorway, appeared my uncle. Suddenly everyone, including the senior military officers, was on their feet, yelling and cheering and applauding. My uncle looked absolutely magnificent. He was wearing a dress uniform, and his chest was covered with medals. For what seemed like a long while he just stood in the plane's doorway, smiling at the crowd and waving. Despite myself, I was crying uncontrollably.

The rest of the day was a blur. I remember that one of the generals approached the access ramp to the plane and saluted, and Lloyd saluted back. Before long, Lloyd was sitting in the place of honor behind the podium, while officer after officer spoke of how the direction of the war was now changing in our favor. They emphasized that the information Lloyd and Captain Gause had provided to General MacArthur would be crucial in helping us turn back the Japanese tide, and their incredible escape from the Philippines proved that American servicemen could survive any difficulty. For me, the highlight of the day was when one of the generals said, "This day proves how every American has a role to play in the war effort. Not only do we honor Captain Osborne for his heroism, but also present today is his mother, Private First Class Grace Osborne, who is playing a crucial role in enabling thousands of American women to contribute to our effort to win the war." He then invited Gracie to join Lloyd at the podium, and the resulting news photos of mother and son in uniform, arm-in-arm, were seen by millions of Americans around the country the next day.

My uncle closed the ceremony with some brief words of thanks to all who had gathered to welcome him home. Once the swarm of people who surrounded Lloyd to shake his hand and slap him on the back had dispersed, our extended family was driven back to our Orange Grove complex. Some thoughtful person had arranged an "off-limits" barrier around our apartments so we would not be hounded by the press day and night. After Lloyd and my grandmother had changed into civilian clothes, all of us sat down to a wonderful meal that had been catered by the Army.

Suddenly Lloyd was no longer the impressive war hero but the same loveable uncle he had always been—funny, mischievous and clever. My grandmother also shed her military persona and behaved as the strong, caring mother figure we were all familiar with. Somehow we all knew not to ask about the war or Lloyd's recent harrowing experiences, but to talk about what life was like for us here at home. Lloyd had always been a great fan of UCLA sports, and he wanted to know how the football team was shaping up for the new season and how the tennis team had done. My grandmother wanted a blow-by-blow account of what I was up to, and she quizzed each member of our family on how they were helping to raise me.

One morning not long after Lloyd's triumphant return, an Army car arrived to take Lloyd and Gracie downtown for briefings. When they returned, my grandmother told us that she was "needed" for a new duty and could only stay with us for one more day. Lloyd told us that the Army wanted him to go on a national recruiting tour. He would speak to local newspapers and radio stations around the country, telling of his exploits in the Philippines and his incredible escape, and encouraging skilled young men to volunteer for duty. After several more days of fun and relaxation with the extended family, Lloyd once again donned his military uniform and was picked up by an Army car. We didn't see him again for many weeks, though the Army frequently sent us clippings about him from around the country.

After several months, Lloyd returned from his recruiting trip. He told me that the Army wanted him to spend the rest of the war recruiting on the home front, but he actually hated doing that kind of work while so many others were in combat around the world. He had sent a strong and personal message directly to General MacArthur, asking to be reassigned. Lloyd laughed as he told me, "Most officers dislike MacArthur because he has the world's biggest ego, and everything is always about him. On the other hand, he took me under his wing when we were in Australia, and we spent a lot of time together. Despite his flaws, he really is an infantry guy." For Lloyd, this was a high compliment. My uncle then whispered conspiratorially to me, as he frequently did, "I know that Damon Gause has been pestering MacArthur to get him back into combat. Gause and I never got along—as a matter of fact, we fought about almost everything—but one thing I've never doubted about Damon is his courage. He is one very brave guy, and in all the months we were together in that little boat, he was never afraid of anything, not even death. My bet is that MacArthur will get him assigned to Europe to get Gause out of his hair. I also plan to approach MacArthur for an assignment somewhere in the middle of the action."

Looking back, neither Lloyd nor I had any idea of what lay ahead for him or the rest of our family in the weeks and months ahead. Perhaps if we had known, we would have been less celebratory, more solemn. But that is a story for another day.

POSTSCRIPT

Dear Reader:

The Los Angeles of late autumn 1942 was a dramatically different city than it had been a year earlier. Now "the War" was with us every minute of every day. It seemed that there were military personnel everywhere, on the streets and in stores and being interviewed on the radio and in the newspapers. Some Army and Navy personnel were assigned to protect the city from invasion, but thousands more were in transit to the Pacific theater, with days or weeks off before their final departure for warfare and possible death. In Los Angeles we soon became particularly aware of the horrors of war, because L.A. became a major hospital center for badly injured soldiers, sailors and airmen. Many days, the front pages of our newspapers would show the arrival of another hospital ship in L.A. Harbor, and day and night one could hear ambulances, sirens wailing, rushing up Fairfax on the way to hospitals throughout the city. Yet by the end of 1942, there was a sense of euphoria and total commitment to winning the war. Many Hollywood stars were visibly participating in the effort—raising money for war bonds, entertaining troops, or heading off on USO tours. Everyday citizens were also eager to contribute. On the evenings that I accompanied Commie on his Civil Defense rounds, the despair and discouragement of spring and summer had now turned to hope and activity. Victory Gardens were being planted everywhere. Rationing was accepted and encouraged. Blackouts were scrupulously adhered to. Even those who had been uncooperative before were now complying with the requirements, although in a few cases with a sort of grudging acceptance.

I began this memoir by describing how I believed myself to be an orphan. Sometime during this momentous year, I learned that I was not in a literal sense an orphan, since my parents were very much alive, although I was not living with them at the time. My parents had divorced not long after my birth, and my mother was helping to support me and my grandparents by teaching at a school on an Indian reservation far from Los Angeles. During the year covered by this memoir, I don't recall seeing my mother, but things would change in the months ahead. But that is a story for another day.

At the beginning of this memoir I promised that I would restrict this story to a period of twelve months between late 1941 and late 1942. I will keep that promise for now, even though I realize there is much more to be told about each of the characters in the story. Indeed, in some cases there were twists and turns that changed the lives of our characters forever, in both positive and tragic ways. Perhaps, if time and destiny allow, I can continue the saga, and reveal some of the surprising events that occurred just beyond the timeframe of the current story. And, on that day, I hope I can tell the stories of Charles and his brother, of Ted and her new life and identity, of Commie and his role in the rapid growth of L.A. during the war years, and of Rosita and her surprising participation in the war effort. I also hope I can finish the stories of two incredible war heroes: William Lloyd Osborne, and his mother, Grace Elaine Osborne. Both of them had important and valiant roles yet to play, and both suffered greatly for their valor, but both were rightfully honored for their strength and dedication. To this day I hold their memories dear.

Part II

Late 1942 – Late 1943

PROLOGUE

Dear Reader:

I used to think that I was unusual because my first memories of life were seared so powerfully into my brain; but as I have shared my story with friends and received their feedback, I have learned that early emotions and images hold a special place of strength and clarity for many. Several people told me of painful or unexpected events in their childhood that to this day stand out as among their most vivid memories. The events of December 7, 1941, and the year that followed, are with me today as clearly as they were so many years ago. The horrors of war and the prospect of losing a dearly beloved father figure impacted my life with overwhelming power. From time to time I still awaken, as from a deep and troubled sleep, to hear the uncontrollable sobs of my grandmother, saying over and over, "Lloyd...oh, Lloyd, my son..."

I have shared my experiences of the first year of the war in *Orange Grove Goes to War*, and I am extremely grateful to those who read that volume and provided me with mostly favorable comments and helpful suggestions. I am inspired by the urging of many to continue writing, and to view *Orange Grove Goes to War* as the first part of a more complete memoir of World War II as seen and experienced by a child in Los Angeles. I do believe in the possible usefulness of such an account, since, despite a lot of reading and research, I am unaware of any comprehensive child-eye history of wartime Los Angeles. As I have said elsewhere, my city underwent vast and permanent changes because of the war. I think it is worth knowing how these changes were directly experienced by a young child.

I will try to make the current volume, covering 1943, independent of the previous volume, so that a reader can read one without the other—although, since many of the same characters reappear, a reader may gain greater understanding of the foibles and personalities of the players by reading both volumes.

Despite the vast changes in the character of my city during the first year of the war, my own living arrangements were essentially the same at the end of 1942 as they had been a year earlier, with the biggest difference being that my grandmother had enlisted in the Army and was essentially removed from my life. The rest of my family members, though, were still in place at the Orange Grove complex, where I continued my frequent bicycle circuits around the courtyard.

So, here is the story of the second year of the war as I experienced it, and as it transformed my city in countless ways. I am still haunted by some of the events and happenings of that year, as my life became entwined with those of other children who were refugees of the war, and had experienced things I could not even imagine.

CHAPTER XXIII

The Christmas That Wasn't

Christmas in the year 1941 had taken place largely as normal, despite the recent upheaval of Pearl Harbor and declaration of war: the usual holiday regalia were already in place, most families had already put up and decorated their trees, and retail businesses were already in full "don't skimp on buying expensive toys for the kids" mode. More importantly, the war hadn't yet started to impact people's daily lives: there were no coffins of young soldiers being shipped home, no broken bodies doomed to a lifetime of pain, no rationing, and no constant news of battles lost on the various war fronts. And the carefree California pastimes of sunning at the beach or skiing in the nearby mountains kept people from worrying about a war that hadn't really yet started, and that we were confident would quickly be won. So, despite Pearl Harbor, Christmas 1941 still happened as usual, at least it did for me.

One year later, in December 1942, things were as different as one could imagine. The war had set in with a vengeance and ferocity that our political and military leaders had not expected or adequately prepared for. My own city was especially impacted, because we had a port that received many of the dead and wounded service men. Our hotels were full of families from out of town who wanted to be near their loved ones while they recovered in hospitals and care facilities.

One day in late fall, as the days were shortening and the temperature dropping, Mary Margaret and Rosita sat me down and told me that, due to the grim results of the war and the shortage of resources, my four families had agreed that it would be inappropriate to celebrate the holidays with the usual festive decorations, meals and gifts. Rather than spending time and money on a Christmas tree or presents, we would instead concentrate on helping with the war effort. Due to my work with Commie on his Civil Defense rounds, I was very aware of the seriousness of the war situation, so I could understand why celebrations might seem out of place. However, I still felt a pronounced feeling of sadness over the loss of the Christmas holiday. To this day, as a father and grandfather, Christmas holds a special meaning for me, and I strive to ensure the holidays are as festive as possible for my family, regardless of circumstances.

CHAPTER XXIV

School Days

She was the most completely miserable person I had ever seen. Her eyes were welling with tears, her hands were quivering, and I observed her holding on tightly to her dress, which was dirty and too large for her small body. I had never seen anyone like her, and she tapped into an emotion that I didn't know I had—deep sympathy for another human being, and an immediate desire to reach out to her and relieve her fear in any way I could.

Just moments before, our class had been interrupted by the school principal, who entered our schoolroom with three children about my age. The principal spoke briefly to our teacher, Mrs. Johanson, and then quickly left the room. Mrs. Johanson clapped her hands once, loudly, as she always did when wanting to get our attention. She said, "Class, we have three new children who will be joining us, and I want you to do all you can to make them feel welcome. These boys"—pointing to two stocky, scruffy-looking boys who looked nearly identical and were standing close to one another, holding hands—"are Bogdan and Peter, and they are brothers. And this girl is Sophia. They don't know English yet, so please be patient, and I hope you will help them learn some words." There were a few empty seats at the back of our classroom, and Mrs. Johanson led the twin boys to two side-by-side seats. Then she looked around and, spying an empty seat near the front of the class, led Sophia there. It was just next to my own assigned seat. Mrs. Johanson had obviously seen Sophia's attitude of near-terror and, after making sure Sophia was settled into her seat, she spoke to me and to the girl in the seat just ahead of mine, whose name was Barbara. Mrs. Johanson addressed the two of us in her inimitable "do-it-now" tone of voice, saying, "I want the two of you to make sure that Sophia is…taken care of."

I didn't want to stare at Sophia, but I couldn't help noticing out of the corner of my eye that not only were her hands quivering, but in fact her whole body was shaking, as though she had just emerged from a frigid bath. I could also tell that her breathing was labored—she would inhale quickly, and then hold her breath for what seemed a long time before exhaling. Even without looking directly at her, I could sense a depth of misery and hopelessness I had never imagined could exist. At that moment I made up my mind to do everything I could to help her.

It was somewhat ironic that Mrs. Johanson appointed me as part of a team with Barbara to help Sophia overcome her anxieties, because I was almost as new a student as Sophia was. For reasons unclear to me, but probably having to do with the chaos at the beginning of war, I had never attended school, even though by law I should have been attending for at least a year. But early one morning in January 1943, as the country was entering its second full year of war, after a joyless holiday season, Mary Margaret knocked on my bedroom door and said, "Gary, time to get dressed. Today I'm taking you to school. Your breakfast will be ready in ten minutes." Soon thereafter, she drove me to a school building that I had walked by many times while accompanying Commie on his Civil Defense rounds. The name of the school was Saturn Street Elementary, and its main building was an imposing two-story white brick structure, notable for two carved stone lions on either side of its entrance. The year "1924" was prominently etched on a cement slab just above the main door. Mary Margaret escorted me in, got me registered, and said to me, "Do you know how to get home from here?" I assured her that I did, and she hurried off, leaving me with an elderly female administrator, who asked me, "Is this the first time you're attending school?" I answered "yes," and she said, "Well, I'll put you with Mrs. Johanson. She has a small class, so she can give you a little extra attention." She led me out of her office, down a hallway, and up a set of stairs to Mrs. Johanson's room.

On entering the classroom, I could see I was a year or two older than most of the other kids, and I was certainly the tallest. I'm pretty sure I was the only one who read the newspaper each day. By the end of the first day, despite being new to the class, I was very confident of my status and ability to keep up. My only challenge was that I had rarely interacted with other children up to this point, since I was the only child in my Orange Grove apartment complex and I had no siblings or relatives my age. However, there were a few other kids in Mrs. Johanson's class who I felt comfortable interacting with, including Barbara, who like me was very tall.

The day Sophia and the twins came into my classroom was only a few weeks into the new semester, but our class had already formed a clear group identity. Initially there had been 15 of us, about half of whom were native English speakers, the other half having accents of various kinds; and now with Sophia and the twins there were 18, soon to be 22 as other refugee children came in. I wasn't aware of it at the time, but in retrospect I think many of my fellow students were Jewish, and most of the non-English speakers were likely refugees from Europe. A few minutes after Sophia and the twins were seated, Mrs. Johanson announced, "It's time for Nutrition," which was our mid-morning equivalent of a coffee break, when we were served sweet rolls and fruit juice in the cafeteria. After announcing Nutrition period, Mrs. Johanson quickly came over to Barbara and me and told us, "I want the two of you to take Sophia to Nutrition, and get her something to eat. I'll deal with Bogdan and Peter myself," and she hurried to the back of the class.

I still remember my relief and admiration when Barbara took charge of the situation. The first thing she did was give Sophia a big smile and start talking to her in a confident and friendly manner. We could immediately tell that Sophia understood no English, but Barbara was not deterred, and motioned for Sophia to come with us. We proceeded down the hall to the cafeteria, with Barbara on one side of Sophia and me on the other. Once we had our trays with sweet rolls and juice, Barbara led the three of us to an open table. All the while Barbara kept up a friendly chatter, which seemed to calm Sophia somewhat. When the three of us were seated, Barbara said to me, "Eat your sweet roll and look like you're enjoying it." I did as Barbara instructed, and both of us motioned for Sophia to try her roll. At first Sophia looked at it with suspicion and doubt, but after a minute she took a small bite from the corner of the pastry. She carefully chewed it, and then, to Barbara's and my amazement, devoured the entire sweet roll in three or four large gulps. Barbara and I exchanged looks, and we were clearly thinking the same thing—this girl had not eaten in a long time. Barbara then opened Sophia's carton of apple juice and told her to drink it, while she went back to the counter and managed to obtain another sweet roll, which she brought back to our table and offered to Sophia. Sophia consumed the second roll as quickly as the first. Barbara gave her a big smile and told me to do the same. Our friendliness was not overtly reciprocated, but Sophia seemed more composed, and her trembling had stopped.

Barbara and I repeated our roles at lunchtime. Although the meal was a rather unappetizing plate of soggy pasta with overcooked vegetables, Sophia again ate ravenously. During late morning, after Nutrition, I had noticed Sophia starting to nod off, and when our class reassembled again after lunch, Sophia was obviously having trouble staying awake, especially during an educational movie about "new developments in California agriculture."

When class let out at 3:00 p.m., Mrs. Johanson approached Barbara and me and asked if we could wait with Sophia outside until she was picked up. We readily agreed; however, after 15 minutes of standing in front of the school, no one had appeared, so Barbara went in to tell the principal. A few minutes later Barbara emerged with the principal, who told us she would drive Sophia to the address given to the school as her residence, and that Barbara and I should come along so she could drive us home as well, since it was getting late.

The principal drove to a neighborhood I was not familiar with, behind the famous Brown Derby restaurant on Fairfax near Olympic. The principal pulled up in front of a rundown brown shingle house, and directed the three of us to accompany her as she walked up to the porch and rang the doorbell. A very elderly woman opened the screen door, and seeing Sophia, began speaking very animatedly in a language unknown to us, and motioned for all of us to come into the house. The principal pointed to Barbara and me and gestured to her car, indicating that she needed to take us home, and the woman nodded. Just as we were leaving, Barbara did a very wonderful thing. She took Sophia's small hand in her own, looked directly into her eyes, and said, "Gary and I will see you tomorrow. We are your friends. We will help you. Don't be afraid." Sophia seemed to grasp what Barbara was saying, and she responded with the first word she had uttered that day, and I will never forget my elation and joy at hearing it—she said the word "friend." At that moment Barbara and I both touched Sophia's arm and smiled at her.

In subsequent years I have often thought about Barbara and how, despite her very young age, she was able to reach across barriers of language and culture and life experiences to reach another person's heart. In that moment, when Sophia said "friend," I learned a great lesson about the importance of human social interaction, and in the following months and years I tried to emulate what Barbara had done. I knew that Sophia and the twins, and others I would later meet, had gone through a kind of hell that I could never truly understand. But when I looked into their eyes, listened to their voices, and sensed the profound pain there, that opened a place in my own heart that would be forever reserved for empathy with others' suffering. It is a very quiet place, always sacrosanct, always open.

CHAPTER XXV

The Music Room

About a month after Sophia joined our class at the Saturn Street School, a remarkable thing happened. She had progressed in some ways, particularly in her use of English, but not in others—she was still dressed virtually in rags, her hair was unkempt, and she still seemed very nervous and depressed. Barbara and I continued to accompany her to Nutrition period and lunch every day. As Sophia became better able to express basic thoughts in English, we gathered that her parents had paid someone to smuggle her out of her home country, which we later learned was Poland, and that some Polish people living in New York had put her on a bus to Los Angeles, where she was met by her elderly great aunt. As we already knew, the aunt spoke virtually no English, and lived in an old and rundown house that Sophia now called home. Since leaving Poland, Sophia had heard nothing from her parents or other relatives.

One of our weekly classes at school was Music. It entailed our class trooping en masse down to the music room in the basement and listening for half an hour to recorded music, after which the music teacher would lecture us about the composer or the style. A feature of the music room was a set of cabinets and shelves along one wall, filled with all kinds of instruments—strings, woodwinds and brasses, triangles and castanets. We were told that once we were in a higher grade, we could take lessons in these instruments, and eventually have an opportunity to play in the school orchestra or band. I had noticed that as we listened to music recordings, Sophia would often eye the instruments on the shelves. One day, when we had extra time at the end of class, the music teacher told us we could try out the school's instruments so long as we were gentle. Most of my classmates picked up a small drum or triangle or some other easily playable instrument, but Sophia did something unexpected. She walked directly to the cabinet containing violins and bows, picked one out, and without hesitation, tucked the instrument under her chin, closed her eyes, and began to play. The very first note that Sophia played produced a sound none of us had ever heard. It was deep and strong, pure and utterly beautiful. Every other student, as well as the music teacher, immediately stopped what they were doing and stared intently as Sophia proceeded to play a lovely and magical piece. It was as though an angel had suddenly appeared out of nowhere and invited us to hear a celestial song. I was transfixed by the sound, but I also noticed something else. The person playing the violin was no longer the depressed, sorrowful Sophia; the look in this person's face was serene, now untroubled by the miseries of the world.

Sophia was only able to play for a few short minutes before the end-of-class bell rang loudly, and our class had to return to our regular classroom. Sophia stopped playing, returned the violin carefully to its place in the instrument cabinet, and joined her newly impressed classmates as we made our way down the corridor. Later, during lunch in the cafeteria, some other students came over and spoke directly to Sophia for the first time, telling her how much they had enjoyed listening to her play. Each time one of students spoke to her, Sophia would look down at her plate, not responding, but Barbara, always the most mature, would say something like, "Sophia's a little shy, but thank you for your kind words."

The next week as the class again filed down to the music room, there was an unspoken anticipation about whether we might again have an opportunity to hear Sophia play the violin. Towards the end of class, the teacher smiled and said, "We have a little time before the end of class, so you may play with the instruments if you like." As before, most of us chose a simple noisemaker like a drum or maracas, but we were all watching Sophia out of the corners of our eyes to see what she would do. Without hesitation, Sophia walked to the cabinet containing the violins, selected one, put it to her chin, and just as before, out poured the sweetest, most exquisite sound any of us had ever heard. The rest of us automatically put down our little noisemakers, sat down on the floor, and listened. The sound was so beautiful that some of the girls began to cry quietly. And not just girls—at least one boy also had tears in his eyes, and I don't mind admitting that it was me. Sophia played a lovely song, slow at first, then faster, repeating some of the melodies and then introducing new ones. We couldn't tell whether Sophia was playing music she already knew or improvising, but it really didn't matter. There was a magic to her sound, something I had never heard before and, to be honest, have never heard since. Sophia was transported to a different realm, a different world, and she was taking us along with her. While she was playing, everyone remained silent, and our usual restlessness was stilled. When the end-of-class bell rang, it was probably the first time any of us regretted it.

The following Monday, Sophia was not at school, nor did she appear the following day or the day after that. After her third or fourth absence, Barbara asked our teacher if she knew where Sophia was, but she didn't. After a full week had passed, our teacher told us that she would drop by Sophia's house after school to check on her, and that Barbara and I were welcome to come along. We piled into our teacher's car and drove over to the rundown and shabby house we had visited before. As we approached the front door, we could immediately tell that the house was no longer inhabited. Papers had accumulated on the front porch, the mailbox was overflowing, and the scraggly curtain that had hung in the front window was gone. Our teacher rapped loudly on the door, but we knew there would be no response. The old woman who had been living there was gone, and so was Sophia. I was at a loss for words, but Barbara, ever poised, said, "Sadly, I think we will never see Sophia again."

In the months afterwards, when Barbara and I were chatting about something, out of the blue she would muse, "I wonder whatever happened to Sophia. I really hope she found happiness somewhere." I would just nod, with a lump in my throat.

CHAPTER XXVI

Ethel Comes Home

Before the war, my grandmother took frequent opportunities to visit her hometown of Prescott, Arizona. She would load up food in her large old Buick, tell me to hop in, and off we would go. In those days it was considered dangerous to drive during the daytime during the height of summer, so most people driving from Los Angeles to Arizona drove at night when it was less likely that the car's radiator would boil over. A few miles outside of Los Angeles, the highway entered the Mojave Desert—hot, sandy and dusty. After several hours, the road descended into even hotter and dustier conditions, until arriving at the Colorado River. The bridge crossing the river was adjacent to a small California town called Needles, one of the hottest places in the United States, and a rather God-forsaken place in general. During the early 1940s my mother was working as a teacher in Needles, which was the only place she could get a teaching job due to her status as a divorced woman. For the rest of my mother's life, whenever she wanted to conjure up difficult living conditions, she would refer to Needles.

As of January 1943, I had not seen my mother for many months, but she had told Commie and Mary Margaret and Rosita that she would be returning to Los Angeles soon. My surrogate parents were saying things like, "How nice it will be to have your mother back!" Rosita was more merry than usual and chattered to me about "*tu madre*." Especially with my grandmother away on tour, I felt the absence of an immediate mother figure, and I looked forward to my mother's return with great anticipation. Mary Margaret, however, remained silent and pensive as the day approached; she apparently knew something the rest of us did not.

The day of my mother's arrival finally came; it was a crisp Sunday morning in late January, and our families were congregated in front of the complex at the anticipated time. A large, luxurious car pulled up, and we were all eagerly approaching when we got a rather big surprise. My mother got out of the car on the side closest to us, but from the other side emerged a strange man. As a group, we were speechless, not having received any notice that my mother would be with someone. I remember there was a long and very awkward pause while all of us looked at my mother as if for an explanation, and she likewise appeared to be frozen in the moment. The man on the other side of the car did nothing to relieve the tension but simply stood there. Finally my mother cleared her throat, and with a slight tremor in her voice said, "I'd like you all to meet Johnny."

The first to recover his wits was Commie, who walked over and shook the man's hand, which then emboldened each of us to do the same. To say the least, I was very confused as to what was going on and who this person was. My excitement at seeing my mother had dissipated into uncertainty as I looked at this strange man and tried to grasp why he was with her. I wondered whether he would be sharing my bedroom like Lloyd did when he came to visit.

After the awkward introductions, we all repaired to Rosita's apartment, where she had prepared an elaborate dinner. The food was delicious, but conversation was muted. After everyone had returned to their apartments, my mother said to me, "Let's go in and sit with Daddy, and I'll try to explain our new situation." As it turned out, Ethel was intending to live separately with Johnny, which meant that contrary to my expectations and those of my "family" members, I would continue to live with my grandfather at Orange Grove, while my mother and Johnny lived elsewhere.

* * *

Initially I was more confused than upset by my mother returning on the arm of a strange man. As far back as I could remember, Ethel had never truly been a mother to me in the sense of what mothers and children usually experience together, so I had no particular expectations of what that relationship should be. I soon became very upset, however, at the response of my caregivers, who clearly considered that some kind of betrayal had taken place. The angriest was Rosita, who was frequently muttering to herself and hugging me more than usual. As usual, I didn't understand exactly what she was saying, but it was clear that she was fuming. Her husband Homer told me that Rosita had vowed to make up for what she considered my mother's dereliction of duty, and he said that he also would redouble his efforts to help me with my homework.

Soon after settling into her new apartment with Johnny, my mother did start coming over to the Orange Grove complex almost every day. She usually arrived around lunchtime and stayed until late in the afternoon. However, it wasn't for me that she came to visit; rather, she was taking time to be with her father. She would arrive, make a cup of tea for herself and a glass of milk for me, then go into the living room where my grandfather spent almost all of his time. She would sit down on a little hassock, pull herself up close to her father, and begin talking to him in a quiet, peaceful voice. I couldn't make out much of what she was saying since she spoke so softly; but it was obvious that my grandfather listened carefully to her words and that he loved being with his only daughter.

Each time my mother visited, she would also spend at least a few minutes with me, usually taking me into the kitchen and sitting me down at our little breakfast table. I very much liked the way my mother treated me, almost adult to adult, similar to how Charles and Commie treated me. Because we had no previously established dynamic, we were free to create our own new relationship. I appreciated being treated as a responsible, capable young person, and when my mother spent time with me, we would discuss family issues or my health or school, rather than playing little kids' games. After a few minutes of talking, my mother would get up to leave and tell me she looked forward to seeing me the next day.

I don't recall my mother ever preparing meals for me; I guess she was relying on my other "family" members to do that. Yet I don't remember wishing that she would be more of a mother to me; rather I recall being deeply gratified by my mother's tenderness towards her father. My love for my mother was enhanced by seeing her deep devotion to her daddy, and I wouldn't have wanted it any other way.

CHAPTER XXVII

The Brown Derby

One evening a few days after my mother's "betrayal," Commie came noisily into my living room where my grandfather and I were listening to the radio and said, "I have great news. The head of our Civil Defense region has given me an additional territory; now I have a whole block on Fairfax to monitor, and I'll definitely need your help."

A few nights later, Commie showed up with all his Civil Defense regalia and told me to quickly put on my "Junior Defense Assistant" outfit. I always kept my Defense coat ready, and I was dressed almost as soon as Commie had finished talking. As I was following Commie out the door, he told me that we were going to initiate monitoring of our new territory on Fairfax Avenue. The area was a business district with many restaurants, bars and little shops, and it soon became obvious that this was going to be a different type of challenge than visiting individual homeowners to ensure they weren't "leaking light" to the Japanese bombers who might be preparing to destroy our city. With just a few points of light visible from above, potential targets could be "triangulated" with great precision, so it was vitally important that all individuals and business comply with blackout requirements.

One of the first challenges we experienced was with a well-known restaurant, the Brown Derby, which was operating as though there was no war going on. It was brightly lit, and music was blaring. Worst of all, cars were pulling up in front of the restaurant with their headlights on and idling while they dropped off elegantly dressed customers.

Commie was visibly aghast. He charged through the main door of the restaurant into the reception area, grabbed the host by the lapels, and yelled into his face, "Don't you know there's a war going on? This place can easily attract hundreds of Japanese bombers, which would make Pearl Harbor look like a tea party." The host was utterly taken aback and, looking at Commie's official-looking regalia, said, "I'll get the owner." Extricating himself from Commie's grip, he disappeared into the back, and almost immediately an old man came out. Commie read him the riot act about federal and state regulations and blackout rules. Commie had a way of making his points with great emphasis. I said nothing but observed how seriously Commie took his job, and how dangerous our situation actually was in terms of survival of an attack.

In the ensuing days Commie and I continued our Civil Defense work, very successfully in the residential areas, but always struggling to get the restaurants, bars and shops along Fairfax to comply. Commie had been proud to be designated as the Civil Defense captain of Fairfax, but when he actually had to deal with bar owners and other uncooperative businesses, it became clear that his new responsibility was going to be quite a burden.

CHAPTER XXVIII

Lloyd's Escape Plan

I had never seen Lloyd so angry. He was almost hopping up and down, like a small child that has been denied a favored toy. Ordinarily Lloyd didn't like to express anger in front of the adult members of our family, especially his mother, preferring to maintain his image as always in control and never letting daily annoyances get the better of him. In addition, he didn't have anyone that he felt comfortable confiding in, except to a limited extent me. Despite the difference in our ages, we had always been honest with each other, and he had often told me things that he said would be better for only the two of us to know. This was certainly true of Lloyd's campaign against any and all policemen, especially those who would prevent him from driving around L.A. in his preferred freewheeling manner.

Lloyd had just come home on a three-day pass, at the end of which he would have to return to his current recruiting assignment. When Lloyd was home with us, he would spend part of his time at his girlfriend Lee's apartment and part of the time in our Orange Grove apartment with my grandfather and me. When Lloyd was home, he made sure that he and I spent as much time together as possible. He knew that my real father was not part of my life, and he happily accepted his role as a surrogate dad, but with a special proviso that at times he could also be sort of an older brother, and that we could conspire together.

"Boise!! Can you believe that? Boise! In Idaho, of all places! Can you believe they actually want me to stay up there for six months?" Each time Lloyd said the word "Boise" he made it sound as though he was describing one of the lower levels of Milton's Hell. He went on to explain that his current commanding officer was himself from Idaho, that he had set a goal of making Idaho the state with the highest per capita percentage of U.S. Army enlistments in the country, and that he had selected Lloyd as the man to sign up as many Idahoans as possible. Even though the draft was already bringing in thousands of young men, there was often intense competition among the services for recruits, and the Navy and the Marines both carried a certain glamour that the Army lacked. So it was Lloyd's job to convince the young men of Idaho that the United States Army was the right choice for them.

Lloyd was a valuable commodity for the Army because, in those grim early days of the war, there were only a few authentic heroes, and he was one. His incredible escape from the Japanese-occupied Philippines after the Bataan Death March, and his improbable voyage across hundreds of miles of Japanese-patrolled waters with fellow escapee Damon Gause, had been captured in countless newspaper articles and radio interviews. Both Lloyd and Capt. Gause had spoken to Rotary Clubs, church groups and public meetings hundreds of times. Both men had become celebrities, and the Army had decided that their most valuable role would be in recruiting. However, both Lloyd and Gause hated that kind of work and set out to return to combat, despite the fact that both had already come very close to death many times.

"Gary, you can't imagine what Boise is like," he continued. "It's probably the dullest place on earth. Up there, everybody follows the rules, there's absolutely no nightlife, and you can cut the sincerity with a knife." Lloyd's anger was dissipating as he graphically described the horrors of Boise. "The only thing that makes it bearable is the thought that Gause has it even worse, down in Georgia. He writes me all the time, telling me how much he hates recruiting, and his letters always make me laugh, because I know Gause so well, and I can just imagine him fuming and fussing and kicking things. Gause hasn't had any more luck than I have in getting reassigned. But I'm pretty sure one of us will succeed soon, and then the other one will too." Lloyd and Gause had fought with each other since the day they met, but underneath the arguments and sometimes physical struggles, they had great respect for each other. Lloyd was a dyed-in-the-wool infantryman, and had a certain contempt for sailors ("mostly dumb as catfish" he would tell me) and pilots ("think they're demigods just because they can steer a plane"); and Gause was a fighter pilot. But they were in many respects alike—small of stature, cocky, argumentative, resentful of authority, quick to anger. Both were also highly competent, totally loyal to their country, and willing to die for their fellow officers.

Lloyd said to me, "Come on, let's go get an ice cream, and I'll tell you my secret plan." I hopped into the passenger seat of Lloyd's Plymouth convertible, and we headed off toward Wilshire and the Farmers Market, which was one of Lloyd's favorite hangout spots. We sat down at an outdoor table, and Lloyd ordered himself a sundae and me a vanilla milkshake. He spoke to me in a conspiratorial way, saying, "I've sent four or five letters to General MacArthur, but I know how his staff works—he has these guys who screen out things they think the general shouldn't be bothered with. So I'm guessing MacArthur hasn't actually seen any of my letters yet. But I've got an idea for how to get a letter to him directly. I just found out that one of my ROTC pals from UCLA has been assigned to MacArthur's senior Army-Navy liaison staff. As you know, the general took me under his wing when Gause and I arrived in Australia, and he told me that if I ever needed anything, I should let him know. So I'm going to write a very strong letter reminding him of his promise, and give it to my friend, and I'm hopeful my friend can get my letter directly into the general's hands. I recently found out that a new secret unit has been formed to fight behind enemy lines in Burma, and that's exactly where I want to be. I'm going to ask MacArthur to assign me to that unit as soon as possible." Lloyd got a huge smile on his face and said, "Then I'll be able to escape Boise forever!"

CHAPTER XXIX

The Memorial Service

With my grandmother away from home and my grandfather drifting more and more into his own world, I never knew from night to night where I would be sleeping. Most often it was in my own bedroom, but sometimes it would be in the apartment of Rosita and Homer, who had a very comfortable sofa in their living room, and sometimes with Mary Margaret and Commie, who had a guest room that was seldom occupied. The only place I never slept was in Ted and Charles' place, because Aunt Fan occupied their second bedroom, and also because of Charles' drinking issues. By far my favorite place to sleep was on Rosita's couch, because in the morning she would awaken me with a cheerful Cuban wake-up song and urge me into her kitchen, where she had made a delicious breakfast of scrambled eggs, beans and rice, and a cup of steaming hot chocolate. While I ate, Rosita would chatter happily to me in Spanish, only a few words of which I could understand, and then she'd push me out the door with a heavy lunchbox filled with tasty treats, which I looked forward to sharing with my friends.

I had been sleeping on Rosita's couch for a week or two, and was just on my way to school, when Mr. Seiter's limo pulled up unexpectedly. Mr. Seiter hopped out of the back door, caught sight of me, and said, "It looks like you're on your way to school. How about if I give you a ride? I need to talk to you about something." I immediately agreed, and joined Mr. Seiter in the luxurious "conference room" in the rear of his limo. There was one other person there, a young man I had never seen before. Mr. Seiter said, "We don't have much time, and I need to ask you a favor, so let me get right to the point. There was a very great composer who just died last week, and I had worked very hard to get him to compose some music for a film I'm working on. I never got him to agree, but I think I could use one of his piano pieces, which would be perfect for my film. However, I would need to get the rights, and they're now controlled by his widow. She's known to be very family-oriented, so I want to attend the memorial service with my brother and his family, which of course includes you and Theodora. I don't know where Charles is, but you always know his whereabouts, and I'm hoping he'll be available to be a part of my family tomorrow." As Mr. Seiter said these words, a chill went down my back, because I had seen Charles being dumped off at our complex early that morning, which meant he would be in the early throes of recovery from his deep drunken adventures. Mr. Seiter and I had always been very honest with each other when it came to Charles, so I said, "I hate to say this, but he just came back this morning." We both knew what that meant. We were now at my school, and Mr. Seiter took my hand in his in a kindly fashion and said, "I believe we can make this work. Tomorrow morning I'll bring my two best makeup men over to get Charles as ready as possible for the big event." Then Mr. Seiter looked me straight in the eyes and said, "As always, I count on your help."

The next morning, which was a Saturday, I took care to dress in my most elegant dark suit, which Charles had bought for me during one of his fatherly periods. At the designated time that Mr. Seiter had said he would pick us up, I went out to the courtyard to wait for what might emerge from Charles' apartment. After a few minutes, the door opened, and there stood Charles, supported on both sides by Mr. Seiter's makeup men. As the sun hit Charles directly in the face, I thought he was going to fall backwards from the shock of the bright light; but the two makeup men held him up, and I couldn't help myself from laughing. Charles had been made up so heavily that he looked like a kewpie doll and was almost unrecognizable. The two men half-carried, half-dragged Charles down the walkway to where Mr. Seiter's limousine was waiting for us, and I got in with my aunt Ted. Nobody spoke until one of the makeup men said to me, "When we get to the memorial park, you'll hold Charles' hand on one side, and I'll be on the other side. By the way, my name is Tex, and it's a pleasure to meet you," and he reached across and shook my hand. It later turned out that Tex was a famous creator of makeup and disguises, but I doubted he had ever accomplished anything like presenting the brutally hungover Charles as a human being.

When we arrived at the memorial park, high up in the Hollywood Hills, there were numerous fancy limousines parked nearby, and a very elegant-looking gathering of people. I didn't recognize any of them, but Tex whispered to me, "This is a gathering of truly great composers and musicians. I hope Mr. Seiter's plan will work." As we got out of the car, Tex said to me, "You hold Charles' hand, and hold it tight. If he starts to waver, tell me, but your job is to be his attentive son. Never mind the little noises he makes." Charles had not spoken a word since emerging into the sunlight back at Orange Grove, but had been making strange gurgling sounds. I did as I was told and held Charles' hand tightly, and we walked—actually, were more or less carried by Tex—to the site of the service and were seated there by an usher. The service began, and several speakers made dramatic statements about how great this composer had been. I had never heard of him, not being trained in classical music; but it was obvious that this man was highly esteemed.

After all the speeches had been delivered, someone came over to Mr. Seiter and spoke briefly with him, and the next thing I knew, Mr. Seiter, Charles, Ted, Tex and I were standing together with an older gray-haired woman who clearly had been crying. Mr. Seiter said, pointing to me and Charles, "We're great admirers of your husband and would love to honor him in any way we can." It crossed my mind that Mr. Seiter really wanted to use some of this composer's music. At this point, the widow looked directly at me, and she said, "What is your name, young man?" At this point I was much taller than average for my age, and I loved opportunities like this to display my maturity. So I responded to the widow with my name, and told her how much our family (looking now at Charles, Ted and Mr. Seiter) loved her husband's music, and I thanked her for the beautiful service. She smiled at me appreciatively, and I thought, "Mission accomplished." Mr. Seiter gave me a wink.

On the drive back home in Mr. Seiter's limo, Tex told funny stories about life as a makeup man and laughed about how he had managed to create something presentable from Charles' deplorable state. "You should have seen him; he could barely stand up; he couldn't speak—but we fixed him up right!"

I don't in fact know whether William Seiter was ever able to use the music of Sergei Rachmaninoff in any of his films. But I hope so.

CHAPTER XXX

The Banka Island Massacre

I hadn't seen my grandmother for several months, although every week or so she would send me a short letter, saying that she was well and that she hoped I was "obeying my grandfather" (which was ironic because my grandfather never told me what to do). She always said something about how she hoped I was "being productive," which was always high on her list of desirable traits. Before my grandmother had gone off to war, one of her lesson plans for me involved learning the geography of the world. I had inherited my uncle Lloyd's old atlas, probably from when he was in high school, and my grandmother would quiz me on the names of obscure countries, far-off seas, and strange-sounding cities ("find Bhutan, and tell me what countries it borders," or "show me the Aral Sea"). One time when she was home on leave, my grandmother told me she would try to give me a clue in her letters as to what part of the world she was in by including the phrase "Mr. X sends his regards," with "Mr. X" referring to some place we had looked at together while studying the old atlas. Sometimes I could figure out where she was, but usually her clues were too obscure for me, even when I carefully searched through Lloyd's old atlas.

It was a warm evening in early August when my grandmother unexpectedly came into the apartment she and I and Patrick shared. She told me to quickly notify our other families that she was just passing through, but that she wanted to see all of us, even if only briefly.

Within a very few minutes, all of my "mothers and fathers" had joined us in our living room. Even Aunt Fan was there, although Ted was off on a "filming" assignment as usual. I quickly came to realize that my grandmother looked and sounded different. She was more serious, and I seemed to detect a sadness in her voice.

When we had all seated ourselves on chairs or the couch or on the floor, she began speaking. She said, "I only have a few hours to spend with you because I'm passing through. But I wanted to tell you all something of what I'm doing. Although the Army has said my work is secret, and that I must not tell even family what I'm doing, I've learned that much of what the Army tells me to do is nonsense, and so I don't hesitate to tell you all about my real work.

"The Army has transformed the WAACs into the WACs, so we are no longer an auxiliary. We are full-fledged soldiers. My formal title now is 'Morale Officer,' and I'm preparing girls coming directly out of basic training for what they may encounter, advising them on how to cope with the miseries of war. Most of the girls I work with are combat nurses or forward base stenographers. In both cases, these girls are exposed to combat-like conditions and are always in jeopardy of injury or death. As I'm sure you know, the war is taking place in the South Pacific, on islands covered with jungles, steaming hot all year, in many ways barely livable. Our girls are from places all over the country, but no one has been exposed to hellish environments like those found at Guadalcanal or the Solomon Islands. The girls have toughened up during basic training, but toiling on a sweltering, jungle-covered island is very different from being in Georgia.

"I always tell the girls the story of the Banka Island Massacre, when Japanese troops overran a forward base just north of Australia. They separated out all of the nurses, 25 in number, marched them to the beach, and thereupon shot them all in cold blood. That's the enemy we're up against, that's the evil we face every day, and that's what may be in store for any or all of us. But then I tell the girls the story of my own experience with the first cohort of WAACs, and how the trainers expected most of us to fail the training regimen. The fact that every single one of us made it through has inspired me and other soldiers I've known."

At this point my grandmother paused and looked around the room. All of us were in utter and complete awe of her strength and resolve. Of course, we knew she had lied about her age to get into the Army in the first place, and had been told by training sergeants that she would never make it through the program, but she had emerged as a leader.

My grandmother was accompanied by a second lieutenant, whom she described as her "chaperone" and who had been standing quietly in a corner while Gracie addressed us. It was getting quite late at this point, and my grandmother said to her chaperone, "Shall we be on our way? I know we have a plane to catch." The second lieutenant replied, "Private Osborne, whatever you say, I gladly accept. But it is indeed getting late." My grandmother then told all of us, "I hope I'll see all of you again soon. I wish I had more time to spend with Gary, but I'm depending on each and every one of you"—and with this she looked around the room—"to be Gary's caretaker, parent and coach. I know I can count on all of you, and I love you very much." At that point she put on her

Army hat and, accompanied by the second lieutenant, she was out the door.

This was to me the most dramatic and memorable of any of my grandmother's infrequent visits. And it burned her image into my heart, an image I carry with me to this very day.

CHAPTER XXXI

Lloyd's New Assignment

One fall afternoon after school, as I walked up the stairs to the second floor of our apartment, I was greeted by an unexpected sound; it was Lloyd, and he was singing. Lloyd never sang, as he had zero interest in music, so I knew something was up. I opened the door to the bedroom that we shared when Lloyd was on break from his military assignments. Lloyd turned quickly, spotted me, and yelled, "Smatzen!"—his nickname for me. "I have the greatest news of all time." I had seldom seen Lloyd so full of joy. He had just taken a shower and was getting dressed, and he said, "Let's go up to the Farmers Market, and I'll buy you a treat and tell you the news."

Lloyd scurried out the front door, with me a few steps behind. He jumped into his Plymouth convertible—he always jumped in; he never opened the door—and within seconds we were off, speeding up Orange Grove towards the market. Before I knew it, we were sitting at an outdoor table at an ice cream stall, and he was ordering sundaes for both of us. When our ice cream came, Lloyd grabbed my arm and said, "Listen to this. You remember a few weeks ago I told you that an old ROTC buddy of mine from UCLA had been assigned as one of MacArthur's staff officers? At the time, I had just heard via the grapevine that the Army was organizing a jungle infantry unit, which would be perfect for me. So I wrote the strongest letter I could, reminding the general what he had promised me when he honored both Gause and me with Distinguished Service Cross medals. Thank God my letter actually found its way to the general's hands. In this case, the grapevine was accurate, and something called "Operation Galahad" had just been organized, and a commanding officer had already been selected. The timing couldn't have been better for me, because the commander was looking for battalion commanders with experience in jungle warfare. Soon thereafter I was called into a meeting at L.A. Army headquarters, and was told that I'd be receiving new orders in a short period of time, and that my days as a recruiter were over!" As he said this, he clapped his hands and chortled. "Now all I have to do is take Lee up to Boise so we can vacate our apartment, and burn all the recruiting brochures, and get the hell out of that miserable place." As I enjoyed my sundae, Lloyd continued, "This is exactly what I wanted. I want to be where it matters. I want to be where my skills are used." At this point he rubbed his hands together and said with relish, "Smatzen, I can't wait!"

* * *

A few days later my mother was sitting with my grandfather, speaking quietly to him, and I was finishing some homework, when Lloyd burst noisily through the front door. He said, "I'm back! No more Boise! Hi, Dad! How you doing, Sis?" (Lloyd always called my mother "Sis.") "Smatzen, I see you're doing homework, which is good. Finish it up, because I have some things to tell you all." At that, he headed up the stairs to our shared bedroom, and I heard him scurrying around. Within a few minutes he came back into the living room with a large pile of papers in his arms. Looking at both my mother and me, he said, "I want to show you where I'll be. Supposedly it's top secret, but in the Army, nothing's ever really secret, so you might as well know." At this point, he unfurled a very large map of Burma, showing roads, railroads, cities, towns and natural features.

At this point my mother said, "I'll get the details from Gary later, but right now Johnny's waiting for me," and with that she left. My grandfather was starting to doze off, so the map readers were just Lloyd and me.

Lloyd pointed to a spot along the southeast edge of the map and said, "This is where the Burma Road enters from India." With his index finger he traced the two parallel lines indicating the road, which ran across the entire width and depth of the country to the northeast where "China border" was inscribed. "Right now, the Japanese are starving the Chinese troops, not only in terms of actual food, but also weaponry and other critical supplies. The job of my unit will be to clear that road," pointing to the Burma Road on the map, "so that many hundreds of heavy trucks that are already loaded and ready to go can make the trip from India to China.

"But there's one small problem—the entire road from here to there," pointing first at one edge of the map and then the other, "is occupied by thousands of first-class Jap troops equipped with tanks, artillery and heavy weaponry. We're going to clear the road, the main difficulty being that we can't actually access the road, so we're going to use the jungle on both sides as our combat territory." Lloyd then paused, and with a smirk on his face said, "I can't wait to get started." It was apparent that Lloyd's new assignment would bring unbelievable dangers and frequent risk of death; and he was overjoyed!

CHAPTER XXXII

Wildcatting

Since Lloyd was frequently stopped by traffic cops while driving his convertible at excessive speeds around L.A., he had made a practice of carrying his Distinguished Service Cross medal with him. Whenever he was pulled over by the cops, he would pull out his medal and show it to the officer, who invariably said something like, "Of course I've heard of you, Colonel Osborne; good luck on your next assignment." Lloyd loved that whole process, and it was an additional source of fun for me as his young passenger.

One morning, shortly before Lloyd was to leave for his new assignment, he had driven me to the Farmers Market, where we were enjoying hot chocolate and donuts, when he suddenly said to me, "Smatzen, did I ever tell you how the Osbornes were going to become millionaires?"

I said, "I don't think so, and I believe I would have remembered."

He said, "I have to tell you that story, because…" He paused, and then said, "No, better, I'll show you!" I had no idea what Lloyd was talking about, but he grabbed my arm, pulled me into his convertible, and off we went at top speed up Sepulveda. Lloyd yelled to me over the wind, "Daddy was going to become a millionaire by sinking an oil well up near Bakersfield. I've never shown you the site, but I will right now."

"You're going to take me to Bakersfield?!" I happened to know that Bakersfield was over 100 miles north of L.A.

"Yeah, we'll be there before you know it! We should be in Bakersfield by lunch, and I can show you where the oil well was, because Daddy took me along when we drilled."

All of this was totally mysterious to me; but during the drive, which proceeded at speeds of close to 100 miles per hour, Lloyd explained to me that after his father moved the family from Arizona to California for economic reasons, he decided to try his hand at wildcatting. Lloyd continued, "Daddy did all the calculations in terms of how deep he'd need to drill, how much it would cost, what equipment he would need, and how he would cap the 'gusher' when it came in. In those days it was possible to lease a small piece of land—an acre, I think—from each county for the purposes of oil drilling."

After a remarkably short period of time driving at undoubtedly unsafe speeds, Lloyd pulled off the main highway and drove 20 or 30 miles on backroads to an area that was already populated by some working oil wells. Lloyd explained to me that his dad had leased a parcel of land for a short period of time, perhaps a week, and that he had hired a drilling company to come in and drill on his land. Lloyd told me, "I believe Daddy did everything humanly possible to ensure success, but in those days it was impossible to know exactly where the edge of the oil lake was. It was obvious from the many nearby parcels of land with abandoned equipment that lots of people had tried to drill but come up dry. My approximation is that only one in ten of the previously drilled areas had been successful. Even the parcel that my father leased had two or three unsuccessful holes already in the ground. However, if you struck oil just once, you'd be rich instantly." At this point, Lloyd broke out into a laugh. "I think you'll guess by now that Daddy didn't hit it big. But maybe we're better off as we are."

There were several other men wandering around the oil fields, and one of them looked over when Lloyd laughed, and came over to where my uncle and I were standing. The man said, "So you drilled and came up dry, eh?" Lloyd chuckled and said, "Nope, we hit a gusher, but it only had about six cups of oil, and the rest was water." The other man smiled and gazed out at the many other unsuccessful plots of land and said, "Well, you're definitely in good company. I've been out here a couple of years since my well went dry, with no luck since. That's been the experience of most of us wildcatters."

As Lloyd and I sped back down the freeway towards L.A., I realized that our visit to Bakersfield had somewhat altered my view of my grandfather. I believed that with a little luck, he could have achieved his financial dream, and provided a very different life for his family. I felt a little sorry for him, and realized the deep disappointment he must have felt. However, Lloyd seemed to take things in stride, laughing to me over the sound of the wind, "Smatzen, never become a wildcatter!"

CHAPTER XXXIII

The Last Family Meeting

Normally our extended family meetings were enjoyable for me, since it gave me a chance to interact with my favorite people. However, on this particular morning in late November 1943, as we all gathered in the living room of my apartment, I felt a strain of tension that was unfamiliar to me. Every member of my extended Orange Grove family was present, as was Johnny.

Rosita was sitting next to me on the floor as she often did, so she could "give me lots of hugs," as she would put it. Commie spoke first. "Most of us know that changes are in the offing for our family. But no one has been very specific about what those changes might be, so I've asked Ethel and Johnny to come give us an update on their plans." He then looked at my mother with an unspoken request that she speak. She was obviously very nervous and ill at ease. It occurred to me at the time that the person who should have been speaking was Johnny, but that wasn't his way. He said almost nothing at this meeting or afterwards about their plans.

My mother started speaking. Her voice was quavering. Rosita pulled me closer to her, holding me tightly in case something upsetting should be said. "Johnny and I are getting married pretty soon. You're all invited to participate in some way, except I should say that we're not planning to have a formal wedding ceremony, merely a justice of the peace. And soon thereafter, we plan to move to a house near where Johnny works, along with my mother and father and Gary."

She paused, and unexpectedly Homer spoke up and said, "By the way, we've been wondering why an able-bodied young man like Johnny hasn't yet been drafted. I assume he has what's called an 'Essential Occupation.' Is that true?"

At this, Homer looked directly at Johnny. Johnny appeared to be taken aback at being addressed so directly, but he responded simply, "Yes. I'll explain the details some other time."

All this was news to me, and I believe I was quietly crying at the idea of leaving my familiar house and family, which of course caused Rosita to squeeze me even harder. My mother continued, "War changes many things and affects many families. Before Johnny and I came back from Needles, I never realized what a beautiful family you all had created here for Gary. I now realize that our move to another house will affect everyone in a profound way. I'm truly sorry for that. But whatever Johnny and I can do to keep this family together, I promise you we'll do it."

* * *

In the following days, I found myself experiencing an emotion I had never felt before. Some might have called it depression; some might have called it discouragement; all I knew was I had a deep and abiding sadness in my soul. Each day, I realized, brought me closer to leaving the family I had loved and lived with since the beginning of my conscious life. Since that horrendous day in early December 1941, everything I knew and valued revolved around my caregiving family. It was all I knew, and I valued it deeply. I even loved our Orange Grove neighborhood. On a clear day, the Santa Monica mountains just to our north appeared so close, it seemed like I could reach out and touch them. I had also grown to love my new school, and I valued the trust that had been placed in me by my teachers and the principal to help care for the refugee children who arrived almost daily, having experienced horrors I could never even imagine.

As Homer had correctly surmised, Johnny had an "essential job," which involved work on new kinds of aircraft designed to give America an important advantage in the ongoing war. Northrup Aviation was located just south of Los Angeles, and Johnny had purchased a house on 63rd Street in the southern part of the city. Part of my sadness, I think, came from the number "63." I couldn't comprehend the size of a city that had 63 parallel streets. The highest number street I knew was 8th Street, just a few blocks away, and 63rd Street sounded to me like the ends of the earth.

* * *

When moving day finally came, Johnny rented a small truck, and all my beloved family helped my mother and me pile my possessions into the back of the vehicle. As I held each of my family members tightly in my arms to say goodbye, I did not want to let go of anyone. I'm sure I was crying and feeling bereft, which I still feel today when I think about that separation.

Each one of my caregivers said something special to me as I tearfully held on to them. Rosita, of course, had a lot to say, and though I couldn't understand all of her words, I fully understood her sentiment. Homer spoke more eloquently than usual as he said, "We'll always be your family. Never forget that. We know how much you love us, and how much you've given to us over the past two years. Thank you."

Commie was his usual positive self, and he gave me a huge hug and said, "I'm sure I'll find a good job for you on my sales team. Don't disappear. And never forget who you are."

Mary Margaret said almost nothing; she was whimpering and seemed unable to speak.

Charles said, "You're a New York man now. I'm sending along your fine suits so you look special in your new neighborhood." We held each other for a while, and finally he said, "You and my brother have done a lot for me, and I will repay you, I promise. Not, of course, in money, but in strength and knowledge of the world."

Then, before I knew it, I was sitting between Ethel and Johnny in the front seat of the truck as it pulled out and headed down the street. I didn't want to look back, because my eyes were so filled with tears. I now fully realized, with deepest emotion, that the days of my life with my Orange Grove family were over forever.

Part III

(fragment)
Late 1943 – Late 1944

CHAPTER XXXIV

Running Away

My new house on West 63rd Street was a small, two-bedroom ranch-style home, built only a few years before. It was located on the top of a hill, with one side descending deeply into a gully, the other side abutting gentle hillsides. Those who fly over Los Angeles today can see a grouping of small hills southeast of the Santa Monica Mountains. Then as now, the north-facing side of the hills was called Baldwin Hills, where there were many fancy homes. The south-facing side of the hills, where I lived, was the Windsor Hills neighborhood, which was much less elegant.

Our house had a small front porch. When you entered the house, to the right was a spacious and comfortable living room with a large fireplace; straight ahead was a hallway with a small bedroom, which was mine, and a larger master bedroom where my mother and Johnny slept. On the left immediately upon entering the house was our formal dining room, which we only used a few times a year for special occasions, such as Thanksgiving or Christmas dinners. On the other side of the formal dining room was our kitchen, with a breakfast nook on the left and appliances on the right. At the rear of the kitchen was an enclosed porch with laundry facilities, with a back door that led into a pretty backyard with fruit trees.

Located deep in the backyard was a small cabin that was to be the abode of my grandparents, once my grandmother got back from the war. For now, I was able to use the cabin as sort of my own private clubhouse. Behind the cabin was a spot where rubbish was burned, and a clothes-drying area. Needless to say, there were many nooks and crannies back there where a boy could hide out, conceal his mischievous projects, and be free from the prying eyes of adults.

Despite the attractiveness of our new house, my first few months living on 63rd Street were a most unhappy period. I had lost my beloved and supportive family at Orange Grove, and I missed the apartment I had shared with my grandfather and Lloyd when he was in town. I had also had to leave the Saturn Street School and, because of some bureaucratic mix-up involving my transfer from one school to another, I was not yet enrolled in a new school. And as it was turning out, Johnny represented no companionship for me; he worked long hours at Northrup and played golf on the weekends, and even when he was home, he expressed little interest in what I was up to. My mother in turn seemed overwhelmed with having a new house to take care of. None of the other families on the block had young children, so there was no one around for me to play with. I remember those early days of 1944 dragging on so painfully that at one point I actually resorted to listening to daytime soap operas on the radio.

But one morning, like a flash of light, I saw my way out: I would run away from home. Perfect! Freedom! New adventures! Of course I had read the stories of Tom Sawyer and Huckleberry Finn, and was familiar with "life on the road," so I set about packing up my few belongings. But then I had to face the dilemma of whether to tell my mother I was running away. On the one hand, I was generally an obedient child, and I would have felt badly simply disappearing without explanation. On the other hand, part of the excitement in running away was exactly that, leaving without telling anyone. I decided that even though it might cause my mother major distress, I should at least tell her I was leaving. It was around lunchtime on my departure day, and I found my mother standing at our dining room table, when I told her, "Mom, I'm sorry, but I have to leave home."

I was expecting some tears, perhaps some clinging on to my clothing as I walked out the door; I had rehearsed it all in my mind so many times. But instead, my mother said calmly to me, "Want me to fix you a sandwich?"

Somehow, this took a lot of the wind out of my sails. The fact that my mother was not only not trying to stop me from running away, but was going to give me food to tide me over, was a big surprise. However, I was in fact hungry, so I said, "Well, I guess that would be nice."

So my mother made me a double-decker ham and cheese sandwich, put it in a bag with an apple and a cookie, and said, "Perhaps you should take an umbrella, in case it starts to rain." I thanked her and went out the back door with my parcels.

I got as far as the little cabin in the backyard when my hunger got the better of me, and I went in, sat on the floor, and ate my sandwich with a satisfied sense that I was now "on my own." After eating my sandwich, I pulled a few comic books out of my satchel and read for a while, greatly enjoying my independence to do whatever I wanted. As the cabin grew warm in the afternoon sun, I became drowsy, so I lay down with my head on my knapsack for a little nap. When I awoke, it was dusk and nearing dinnertime. It didn't seem quite so appealing to head out to parts unknown in the dark, and the thought of a hot meal was quite tempting, so at that moment I decided it would be best to postpone my departure to another day.

The following day, I got distracted with my baseball cards and decided to wait another day. The day after that, I found some other excuse. And so the days passed until my plans to run away receded into the past like a dream. Some months later, while sitting around after school with some of my new friends, I learned that all of us young boys at one time or another had experienced the "eureka" moment of deciding we would run away from home to solve all our problems, and we laughed at how similar our experiences had been. One friend said he had read somewhere that most young boys run away at some point, but only one in a hundred actually get past their own backyard. I was relieved to know I wasn't the only one.

CHAPTER XXXV

A New Life

When we first moved to West 63rd Street, there were no other children on our block. Our house was actually at the extreme edge of the city of Los Angeles; just to the south began the separate city of Inglewood, so children living even one block apart attended different schools, and tended to have separate lives. However, a few months after moving to 63rd Street, I was enrolled at 54th Street elementary school, and my social life took an upturn when my mother befriended a woman whose son, Gordon Ellison, was in my class. He and I became very close friends, riding the bus together to school, and on weekends we liked to ride our bikes as far away from 63rd Street as possible. (As I write this, 70-plus years later, I am happy to say that Gordon is still my friend.)

Gordon and I soon were part of a tight-knit group of friends, including Jan Olsen, whose in-depth knowledge of cars impressed us all, and David Sanderson, whose family owned a prominent Swedish travel agency in Los Angeles. It is today amusing to think of how innocent and well-behaved we all were. I don't recall any of us ever getting into serious trouble over anything, perhaps because we didn't know how, or maybe we just didn't try hard enough.

* * *

Shortly after I had settled into school, my mother decided I needed to study a musical instrument. This was odd to me, because no one else played an instrument in our family. But she was convinced I needed to start music lessons of some kind, and she decided that the violin was the proper vehicle.

In my new neighborhood, it turned out that there were many single men who lived in small studio apartments and made a living by teaching various musical instruments or singing. I was later told that in Europe after World War I, virtually every city of any size had at least one full-size symphony orchestra, and in some cases two or even three. But as the post-war years saw the rise of fascism and anti-Semitism and general disruptions, many orchestras were disbanded, and the individual musicians had to make do. Those who could, immigrated to the United States, and these men became the music teachers of hopeful young students like me.

My teacher was Mr. Rizzo, who I believe had been from Serbia. He was a sad-faced older man, whose tiny apartment was cluttered with musical scores, old and new violins, and a single beat-up upright piano. Mr. Rizzo was nice enough, but I could sense that he didn't see me as a student with much promise. From the beginning of studying with Mr. Rizzo, whenever I would start practicing, I would also start sneezing. I attributed this to the rosin, which when I put bow to string would cause little puffs of yellow dust to rise from the fingerboard. My constant sneezing prevented me from serious practice, so my progress was slow and painful. I remember thinking that it was fortunate for Johnny and Ethel that I had the cabin in the backyard to practice in, since the sounds were pretty unpleasant, even to me who was actually playing.

After a few months of this struggle, I told my mother, "I don't think this is going to work. Whenever I start to play, I have an allergic reaction, and I can tell that Mr. Rizzo isn't sympathetic." My mother seemed somewhat disappointed, but not excessively so, and she said, "Why don't you pick out another instrument you'd like to play, one that doesn't involve rosin, and I'll make arrangements for lessons for you." Relieved, I told her I would like to play a woodwind, as I found their sound to be pleasant and I was inspired by the great swing woodwind players of the day, including Benny Goodman, Artie Shaw and Jimmy Dorsey. We settled on the clarinet, which I knew could be played in both classical orchestras and jazz bands.

My mother found another Eastern European immigrant to teach me clarinet, a few blocks away from our house. My mother sent Johnny out to obtain a decent clarinet for me, which he did. From the beginning, I enjoyed playing the instrument. The only problem working with my teacher was that, being of Eastern European heritage, his primary interest was polka music, which I had zero interest in. The little compositions he assigned to help me learn the instrument were invariably polka style rather than the swing or big-band style I yearned for. I likely would have practiced harder had my teacher had a broader taste in music.

Nonetheless, I spent countless hours during my school years, all the way through high school, playing clarinet (and later saxophone) in bands, orchestras and small jazz ensembles. Most of my friends also played musical instruments, and playing in bands together strengthened the bonds between us. My life as a woodwind player was certainly much richer than my brief life as a violin player had been.

As alluded to earlier, my relationship with my stepfather Johnny was distant, if free of direct conflict. Then, as later, Johnny never shared any activities such as sports, reading, movies, or other typical father-son pursuits with me. Later I came to realize that this moment in my life of learning a musical instrument would have been an ideal opportunity for him to become involved, because his own mother had run a music school in Los Angeles. He and I did listen to music together sometimes, but he never took the slightest interest in my playing.

* * *

Just as my mother felt that a well-rounded young man should play a musical instrument, she also felt it was important for me to have religious training. Not long after we moved to 63rd Street, my mother made an appointment for the two of us to visit the nearest Episcopal church, which was Mt. Calvary on Slauson Avenue. When my mother and I arrived at the church, a handsome young man invited us in, asked us to please sit down in his office, and introduced himself as Father Caldwell. My mother, who was always ill at ease in situations like this, said hesitantly, "Back home, in Prescott—that is, in Arizona—I attended an Episcopal church; and I believe it's time for my son Gary to begin his religious education." I was a bit surprised hearing her words, since our family had never gone to church together, and I knew that Johnny was non-religious. So this introduction of me to Mt. Calvary was unexpected, but not unwelcome.

Father Caldwell said, "Your timing's perfect. We're starting a new Confirmation class in about a week, and young Gary here will fit right in."

My mother, now somewhat more at ease, said, "I'm so happy to hear that, and I know that Gary will work hard to learn all his lessons."

Father Caldwell asked, "I'm just curious; has Gary had any musical education?" My mother mentioned that I had just started lessons. Father Caldwell smiled in approbation and said that his church had a strong musical community, including a choir, which I would be welcome to try out for when I got a little older. It was starting to occur to me that my "free time" was not going to be so free anymore, between music lessons and practice, homework and church activities. However, as it turned out, being involved with the church became a very meaningful part of my life. Soon after that initial appointment with my mother, I started attending Confirmation class every Tuesday evening, and I eventually became an altar boy. The church was quite small, with a regular congregation of perhaps eighty, and Father Caldwell was very kind, so I quickly felt like an integrated member of the community.

* * *

www.ingramcontent.com/pod-product-compliance
Lightning Source LLC
LaVergne TN
LVHW041632060526
838200LV00040B/1551